THE FOUR TERESAS

THE FOUR TERESAS

Teresa of Avila • Thérèse of Lisieux • Teresa Benedicta • Mother Teresa

Gina Loehr

servant

AN IMPRINT OF
FRANCISCAN MEDIA
Cincinnati, Ohio

Unless otherwise noted, Scripture passages have been taken from the *Revised Standard Version*, Catholic edition. Copyright 1946, 1952, 1971 by the Division of Christian Education of the National Council of Churches of Christ in the USA. Used by permission. All rights reserved.

Note: The editors of this volume have made minor changes in capitalization to some of the Scripture quotations herein. Please consult the original source for proper capitalization.

Excerpts from *Story of a Soul,* translated by John Clarke, O.C.D., ©1975, 1976, 1996 by Washington Province of Discalced Carmelites, used by permission of ICS Publications, www.icspublications.org.

Cover and book design by Mark Sullivan
Cover image copyright © Zoom-zoom | Dreamstime.com

LIBRARY OF CONGRESS CATALOGING-IN-PUBLICATION DATA
Loehr, Gina.
The four Teresas / Gina Loehr.
p. cm.
Includes bibliographical references (p.   ) and index.
ISBN 978-0-86716-944-7 (pbk. : alk. paper) 1. Christian life—Catholic authors. 2. Therese, de Lisieux, Saint, 1873-1897. 3. Teresa, of Avila, Saint, 1515-1582. 4. Stein, Edith, Saint, 1891-1942. 5. Teresa, Mother, 1910-1997.
1. Title.
BX2350.3.L64 2010
282.092'2—dc22
[B]

                                                                    2010004660

ISBN 978-0-86716-944-7

Published by Servant, an imprint of Franciscan Media.
28 W. Liberty St.
Cincinnati, OH 45202
www.FranciscanMedia.org

With gratitude to my fifth Theresa

contents

*You shall love the Lord your God with all your heart, and
with all your soul, and with all your mind. This is the great
and first commandment. And a second is like it, You shall
love your neighbor as yourself.*
Matthew 22:37–39

What would you like to ask Jesus? What are the questions weighing on your heart?

Many of us would ask for direction in these troubled times: How should I raise my children in our post-Christian society? How do I protect my life savings, my job, my future in an unstable economy? How can I promote justice for the unborn and the elderly in a culture of death?

Others would seek to understand life's great trials: Why do I have a terminal illness? Why did my son have to die so young? Why was I mistreated by those I trusted most?

Still others would question Jesus about living their Christian faith: What will help me conquer my persistent sins? What vocation are you calling me to? What should I do to become holy?

The saints asked such questions too. Their lives, like ours, involved elements of anxiety, mystery, and uncertainty. Yet they moved forward with Christian confidence, faith, and resolve. Rather than succumbing to the paralysis of fear or cursing the perplexities of the unknown, they focused on those clear and direct "answers" Christ has already given to all of us.

One such answer came when the Pharisees questioned Jesus. Asked to name the greatest commandment, Jesus referred to the Old Testament teaching that we should love the Lord with our whole heart, our whole soul, and our whole mind, and love our neighbors as ourselves. In this he gave us concrete direction regardless of the particular circumstances—or the lingering questions—of our lives. Pope Benedict XVI says this commandment is "all that Jesus asks of us. Whoever does this, whoever loves is a Christian."[1]

When we set about the business of following this central element of Christ's teaching, we fulfill our Christian calling. Everything else is secondary. The *hows*, the *whys*, and the *whats* of life all fall in line behind what Jesus himself told us is most important: the great commandment of love.

The four Teresas—Thérèse of Lisieux, Teresa of Avila, Teresa Benedicta of the Cross, and Mother Teresa—are masters and models of living out Christ's command. These women will be our teachers throughout the course of this book, assisting us in our efforts to embrace our Christian calling. Each Teresa offers enlightenment on one particular element of the great commandments.

Saint Thérèse, the passionate, emotional girl with the simple faith of a child, shows us how to love God with our whole heart. Saint Teresa of Avila, the great mystic who described the soul as an interior castle, teaches us how to love God with our whole soul. The brilliant philosopher and convert to the faith Saint Teresa Benedicta of the Cross offers insight into the command to love God with our whole mind. And Mother Teresa, whose love for others was so constant and so tangible, helps us grow in love for our neighbors.

This book has one chapter on each woman, and all four chapters follow the same pattern: a biographical sketch ("Her Life"), a presentation of direct teaching ("Her Lessons"), and a reflection on applying the teaching to our own lives ("Living the Lessons"). These sections vary in length and emphasis according to the unique personalities of the Teresas and their distinct methods of teaching.

Taken together, the lives and writings of these four women present us with clear, solid guidance for putting Christianity into practice. Once we are rooted in the fundamentals of the faith, the light of Christ can illuminate the details of our lives still obscured by darkness and confusion. But we must put first things first. So let us begin where Jesus began: the commandment to love God with our whole heart.

chapter one

❋ SAINT THÉRÈSE OF LISIEUX ❋
Loving God With Your Whole Heart

It is no longer I who live, but Christ who lives in me.
Galatians 2:20

HER LIFE

Born on January 2, 1873, in Alençon, France, Marie-Françoise-Thérèse Martin was the youngest of Blesseds Louis and Zélie Martin's nine children. Four of Thérèse's siblings had died, however, leaving her with four older sisters, who all doted upon the beloved baby of the family. The Martin family was truly "functional," filled with friendship, generosity, and Christian piety. The parents loved God, each other, and their children wholeheartedly. Within this haven Thérèse experienced unconditional love from her earliest days.

A sickly infant, Thérèse spent her first year at some distance from the family, in the loving care of a wet nurse. Her recovery, strengthening, and eventual return to Alençon led the Martins to treasure her all the more, having feared they might lose yet another child. Once this youngest daughter had returned, Zélie eagerly told tales of the sweet exploits of this little one who was the joy of the Martin family. Both parents showered attention and affection upon Thérèse, especially her Papa, who called her his "Little Queen."

In the written recollections of her childhood, recorded in her autobiography, *The Story of a Soul*, Thérèse speaks with sentimental enthusiasm about these early days of her life. She recalls the intimate bond of loving friendship she had with her nearest sister, Céline. The two young girls spent all their time together and could hardly stand to be separated. Thérèse's devotion to her sister was such that she even preferred to give up dessert rather than remain at the dinner table once Céline had left!

Although she shared a special bond with Céline, Thérèse relished the company of the rest of the family, spending many hours playing games, singing songs, and performing pantomimes. The Martin family also loved to explore the countryside on their leisurely Sunday walks and to make pilgrimages to religious sites. These were days of tremendous joy for Thérèse, filled with youthful adventure, the beauty of nature, and the company of people who loved her dearly.

However, this time of bliss was short-lived. When Thérèse was four years old, her mother passed away.

Loss in the Family

After Zélie's death Louis moved the family to Lisieux. A melancholy fell over them all, which particularly affected little Thérèse. While she controlled most external signs of her grief, she fought a difficult internal battle. Her sensitive heart keenly felt the impact of this sudden emptiness in her life.

Following the example of Céline—who threw herself into the arms of her eldest sister, Marie, claiming her as her new mother—Thérèse also sought a surrogate mother. She chose the next oldest Martin sister, Pauline, with a passionate declaration: Pauline would be Thérèse's "mother" for the next five years, until Pauline left to join the Carmelite order.

This second maternal loss was nearly unbearable for Thérèse. A severe illness soon struck her so violently that her family feared for her life. Thérèse would later credit the Blessed Mother for a miraculous recovery. Her family brought a statue of Our Lady of Victories into her room. As they offered up fervent prayers, asking for Our Lady's intercession, Thérèse looked up at the statue and saw Mary smiling at her. This experience had a curative effect on Thérèse, who quickly resumed her normal activities.

But extreme emotional sensitivity plagued Thérèse into her early teenage years. She had a difficult time socializing with anyone outside of her family. She experienced more personal loss when her one childhood friend abandoned her. This experience taught Thérèse a lesson about the limitations of human love. She was already learning to depend on the only one who would always be with her, loving her unconditionally: Jesus.

Learning to Love Jesus

Under the care of her second mother, Pauline, Thérèse had grown in love for her Lord. Pauline taught Thérèse to turn her heart to Jesus as her first action every morning: She would help dress Thérèse only after she had made this act of devotion and love. The message was not lost on Thérèse. She understood the importance of giving her heart to Jesus, and she did so often throughout the day.

Pauline also prepared Thérèse for her first confession and her First Communion. Pauline would sit her little sister on her lap and talk about all Jesus had done for them. Pauline devoutly taught her sister the doctrines of the faith. Once when Pauline told Thérèse that the priest in the confessional acted in the person of Jesus, Thérèse asked her older sister if she should tell the parish priest that she loved him with all her heart, since it was to God in person that she would be speaking!

Although she was clearly a pious child, Thérèse's passions extended to realms other than religion. Even during these early years she revealed the artistic inclinations that would later produce fifty-four poems, three manuscripts, and eight plays, in which she performed several lead roles. The beauty of nature, the drama of theater, and the mystery of poetry inspired her. Her creative gifts were also manifested in numerous paintings and decorated religious articles, along with beautiful calligraphic cards she made for special occasions.

Thérèse's childhood bedroom displayed the intermingling of her faith and her artistry. This creative hodgepodge of pious objects and curiosities included a small garden and an aviary, a large black cross, along with statues of the Blessed Virgin Mary, Saint Joseph, and other saints. These devotional items were mixed in with decorations of other sorts, including some of Thérèse's drawings and a portrait of Pauline. On a table covered with green cloth rested an hourglass, next to a watch case and an inkwell. Enamored as Thérèse was with the natural world, she saw all of creation as a great work of art, so she also loved to keep an eclectic assortment of vases with cut flowers, potted plants, and baskets of shells.

This diverse and stimulating environment was the product of a girl who, as a small child, had been asked to select a trinket from a basket full of goodies. Instead of picking one, Thérèse had exclaimed, "I choose all!"[1] This became a theme for her whole life: She refused to choose between the things she loved.

Thérèse's artistry went beyond mixing objects, blending colors, and shaping words. Throughout her life she beautifully united many seemingly opposing realities: stability and adventure, romance and religion, simplicity and maturity, humility and confidence, joy and suffering. Hers was a vibrant, dynamic personality that passionately yearned to embrace the wide spectrum of human experience and live life to the full. This was not a self-absorbed, hedonistic thirst for personal pleasure: Thérèse's energetic passion was rooted first and foremost in her love for Christ.

The Imitation of Christ, by Thomas à Kempis, was partly responsible for encouraging this heartfelt devotion in Thérèse. The classic handbook of holiness was one of her favorite books as a child. She liked to memorize passages from the text by heart. Family members tested her by randomly opening the book and having her recite lines from memory, which she was able to do with surprising accuracy. She carried the book around with her, in her pocket during summer and in her muff during winter. After she announced her plans to enter the Carmelite order, her father picked her a little white flower, which Thérèse put in this book for safekeeping, placing it at the chapter entitled "One Must Love Jesus Above All Things."

In spite of these firm foundations, however, the young Thérèse struggled at times to love Jesus above all else. She had trouble moving beyond her oversensitivity. But on Christmas Eve of 1886, she experienced a conversion. Having overheard her father complain about playing Santa Claus because Thérèse (now thirteen) was far too old for it, the sensitive girl had a decision to make: She could either burst into tears or hold herself together in mature self-control. She managed to do the latter. She believed that, by God's grace, she had overcome her excessive sensitivity and melancholy. The journey had begun toward the spiritual maturity that her budding vocation would require.

An Uncommon Calling

Attached as Thérèse was to her surrogate mother, Pauline's attraction to the Carmelite life of prayer and sacrifice could not help but intrigue her. Before Pauline entered the convent, the two girls dreamt about going off together to live as hermits in their own desert. At the time Thérèse didn't realize this was a fitting description of Carmelite life, but after Pauline entered, Thérèse came to understand that Carmel was the desert she longed for. She felt her calling clearly in her heart; she wanted to enter out of love for Jesus. She and Marie and Céline would eventually follow her sister Pauline into the Carmel of Lisieux.

Thérèse's heartfelt desire to spend her life in loving union with Jesus did not find full satisfaction right away, however. She wanted to enter the order when she was fifteen, a year younger than the required age. Her plea met with resistance from many sides, but she persevered. After negative responses from the local Church authorities, Thérèse traveled to Rome with her father to plead her case before the pope.

This journey exposed Thérèse to new people, places, and things. Yet while the pomp and circumstance, art, culture, and natural beauty might have distracted others, Thérèse saw in all of these further confirmation of the goodness of God and the dignity of her vocation. In *The Story of a Soul,* after painting a verbal picture of the natural beauty she encountered in her travels, Thérèse notes that seeing such wonders stirred thoughts of the grandeur of God and the marvels of heaven. Thérèse had eyes to see the constant reminders of her Beloved all around her.

But the main point of her trip was to ask the Holy Father for special permission to become a nun at the age of fifteen, and in this she was disappointed. When the time for their audience finally arrived, Thérèse was told not to speak to the pope, only to approach him and greet him silently. But the vivacious girl couldn't give up this opportunity! She disobeyed the orders, asking Pope Leo XIII for his permission to enter Carmel. He only said that if it was God's will, she would enter.

Apparently it was God's will. Thérèse patiently waited through more delays until ecclesiastical authorities granted her permission to enter the Lisieux Carmel, several months before her sixteenth birthday. Taking the religious name Sister Thérèse of the Child Jesus and the Holy Face, she now anxiously awaited the day of her profession.

In her characteristic romantic fashion, Thérèse created an invitation for this special day, modeled on her cousin's wedding invitation. In it she referred to herself as "little Thérèse Martin, now Princess and Lady of His Kingdoms of the Holy Childhood and the Passion, assigned to her in dowry by her Divine Spouse, from which Kingdoms she holds her titles of nobility—of the Child Jesus and the Holy Face."[2]

Perhaps God allowed Thérèse to see her heart's desire fulfilled at this young age because her life was to be a short one. She lived only nine years as a Carmelite nun before dying of tuberculosis at the age of twenty-four.

Suffering and Perseverance

Thérèse suffered much during her short life. In addition to the loss of her mother, her personal sensitivities, and her painful separation from Pauline, Thérèse also had to witness the humiliating mental decline and eventual death of her Papa. Finally she dealt with the physical turmoil of her battle against tuberculosis and, in the last days of her life, an accompanying sense of spiritual isolation.

In those excruciating last days, Thérèse no longer felt the love of Jesus. In her last conversations she described the intensity of temptation that surrounded her. She confessed to having thought at one point that she might take her own life to end the agony if it weren't for her faith. But she never doubted Jesus' love for her. Even though she was slowly suffocating, she still managed to gasp out words of love and affection for him, right up to the last moment of her life. Because she truly loved Jesus with her whole heart, she wasn't dependent on the experience of consolation.

Thérèse believed her mission of bringing souls to love Jesus would really begin only after she had reached her eternal home. She once said, "The things the good Lord has in store for me after my death, and the glory and love I foresee, so greatly surpass all that can be conceived that I sometimes have to stop my thinking, for it makes me dizzy."[3] When her sister Marie expressed the sorrow the sisters would feel when Thérèse died, she replied, thinking of her mission, "Oh, no, you will see; it will be like a shower of roses."[4]

Countless people have witnessed this shower of roses. Saint Thérèse of Lisieux was already a phenomenon within a few years of her death, because her message moved so many people, and many also felt the tangible effect of her prayers. Thus the Little Flower came to bloom in her full beauty and fragrance.

HER LESSONS

Pope John Paul II declared Saint Thérèse a doctor of the Church in 1997. Her teachings on love are part of the legacy that earned her the title. But Thérèse's teachings were never scholarly or academic; they were simply the insights she gained through prayerful reflection on her personal experiences.

The Gift of Love

Thérèse's understanding of the significance of love, for example, grew in part out of her experience of longing to do *everything* for Christ. She had felt the yearning not only to be a Carmelite, a spouse, and a spiritual mother but also to be a missionary, a warrior, a priest, an apostle, a martyr, a crusader, and a papal guard, among other things. In reflecting on the various parts that make up the body of Christ, Thérèse saw herself in *all* of them.

But Thérèse came to an important realization when reflecting on First Corinthians 14, which explains that all the greatest gifts are nothing without love. This led Thérèse to understand that *love* enabled the apostles to preach and the martyrs to make their great sacrifices. *Love* kept the body of Christ alive in the world. She wrote in her autobiography, "I understood that love comprised all vocations, that love was everything, that it embraced all times and places.... In a word, that it was eternal!"[5]

Saint Thérèse embraced the truth that loving Jesus is the goal of life and our most important task. She said, "There is but one thing for us to do...and that is to love, to love Jesus with all the energy of our heart."[6] Her love for Jesus, though deeply passionate, was not purely emotional. It was fundamentally a choice, a response to his love for her. When she no longer felt a tidal wave of romantic sensibility, still her pain and grief did not stifle her love. Hers was an authentic love, not a fanciful illusion, and thus it brought her deep contentment.

Thérèse's approach to concretely living out this love was one of humble simplicity. She referred to it as "the little way."

The Little Way

Five years after entering the Carmelite order, Thérèse began to help form novices. Here she had the opportunity to share with others the little way Jesus had been revealing to her for many years. Thérèse would refer the young sisters to Matthew 11:25: "I thank you, Father, Lord of heaven and earth, that you have hidden these things from the wise and understanding and revealed them to infants."

Thérèse interpreted these words to mean that the smaller and simpler we are, the more gifts God will bestow upon us. Acknowledging that we are like these helpless babes softens our hearts to embrace Jesus. As Thérèse said, "Sanctity…consists in a disposition of heart which makes us humble and little in the arms of God, conscious of our weakness, and confident to the point of audacity in the goodness of our Father."[7]

Jesus loves us not because we're perfect but because he is perfect. Thérèse knew this. Her faults and failings didn't worry her. On the contrary, her weaknesses caused her to rejoice in God's mercy. She progressed in holiness because she didn't wait until she was perfect to begin her journey toward perfection! Her focus was not on what she did but on Christ's initiative and mercy, indeed, on what Christ has done for all of us. This was an important element of Thérèse's great love.

Thérèse believed that when we acknowledge our imperfections and recognize our need for help, we empty our heart of self-love and make room for Jesus. "Let us not leave anything in our heart except Jesus,"[8] she once said.

The Eagles and the Elevator
Throughout *The Story of a Soul,* Thérèse playfully elaborates on the idea of the little way. She uses analogies that range in style from the poetic to the practical. At one point she tells the story of a tiny bird and an eagle:

> How can a soul as imperfect as mine aspire to the possession of the plenitude of *Love*? O Jesus,... You whom I love UNIQUELY, explain this mystery to me! Why do You not reserve these great aspirations for great souls, for the *Eagles* that soar in the heights?
>
> I look upon myself as a *weak little bird....* I am not an *eagle....*
>
> The little bird wills *to fly* toward the bright Sun that attracts its eye, imitating its brothers, the eagles.... But alas! The only thing it can do is *raise its little wings*; to fly is not within its *little* power!...
>
> Jesus, I am too little to perform great actions.... My *folly* consists in begging the eagles, my brothers, to obtain for me the favor of flying toward the Sun of Love with the *Divine Eagle's own wings!*
>
> ...One day I hope that You, the Adorable Eagle, will come to fetch me, Your little bird.[9]

Thérèse considered great saints like Teresa of Avila and John of the Cross to be her "brothers," "the eagles." She imagined that they could soar to divine heights because of their greatness and strength. But she didn't feel she belonged in their company. She saw herself as a very simple soul who was well aware of her limitations and weaknesses. Yet she hoped to soar to the heavens and fully possess the love of Jesus. In fact, her weakness gave her confidence that she would make it to the heights, because she trusted that God himself would take her there. She trusted in his power and strength, not in her own.

Thérèse expanded on this idea using the analogy of a recent invention of her day, the elevator:

> Alas! I have always noticed that when I compared myself to the saints, there is between them and me the same difference that exists between a mountain whose summit is lost in the clouds and the obscure grain of sand trampled underfoot by passers-by. Instead of becoming discouraged, I said to myself: God cannot inspire unrealizable desires. I can, then, in spite of my littleness, aspire to holiness.... But I want to seek out a means of going to heaven by a little way, a way that is very straight, very short, and totally new.
>
> We are living now in an age of inventions, and we no longer have to take the trouble of climbing stairs.... I wanted to find an elevator which would raise me to Jesus, for I am too small to climb the rough stairway of perfection. I searched, then, in the Scriptures for some sign of this elevator,...and I read these words coming from the mouth of Eternal Wisdom: *"Whoever is a LITTLE ONE, let him come to me"* [Proverbs 9:4]. And...I felt I had found what I was looking for.... The elevator which must raise me to heaven is Your arms, O Jesus![10]

Thérèse's littleness was her ticket for the divine elevator. Because God wants the "little ones" to come to him to find help and strength, Thérèse believed that weak and imperfect people needn't despair of reaching the pinnacle of love. Instead their littleness can actually help them find their way. But what exactly does Thérèse mean by "littleness"?

Learning Littleness
In the verse from Proverbs that Thérèse quotes, the original biblical Hebrew phrase for "little one" is *haser lev*. These two words have a range of meanings throughout Scripture. *Haser* usually means to decrease, diminish, strip off, disappear, or be lacking. *Lev* refers to the heart, mind, will, or inner man. As such, the "little one" conveys not so much someone who is small, childish, cute, or stupid but someone who is fundamentally *missing* something. The "little one" has an impoverished heart, an inner self that is decreased, diminished, almost nothing in its obscurity. The little one is, in a sense, unable to even function on his or her own.

This is the idea Thérèse expressed so simply in describing herself as an "obscure grain of sand trampled underfoot by passers-by." She cheerfully contemplated the radical depth of her personal poverty because she wasn't afraid of the truth about human frailty, incapacity, and weakness. She knew how far our shrunken hearts are from being able to love Jesus as we should.

Thérèse recognized the problem and found the solution in Christ. Rather than pretend we are strong, capable, and autonomous, we go to Jesus. We rely on his strength. We let the Divine Eagle carry us on his wings. Thérèse wanted Jesus to do the work for her because she knew she couldn't do it herself. She threw herself into his arms with all the trusting innocence of a child.

Thérèse is a model of that childlike faith Jesus referred to when he said, "Let the children come to me, and do not hinder them; for to such belongs the kingdom of heaven" (Matthew 19:14). Thérèse's faith wasn't childlike because of *childishness* in her personality; rather her faith was childlike because it radiated complete trust, confidence, and loving surrender, rejoicing in her Father's presence and power. So, too, her special love for the Christ Child wasn't based on how cute and sweet baby Jesus was but on the radical humility of the Incarnation and the unfathomable love of a God who gave us the perfect model of humble obedience. The Little Way is rooted in a profound understanding of both our weakness and God's strength.

Thérèse's passionate nature was extravagant in its love and trust. She never feared that she would run out of confidence or that Jesus' love for her would come to an end. She knew that God was rich in love and mercy. And because she attached herself to him with such devotion, she had an abundant share of his heavenly wealth.

Complete Confidence in Christ
Thérèse's earthly father was gentle, generous, and holy. Thérèse loved her Papa dearly and never doubted his love for her. This helped her develop confidence in the goodness of her eternal Father as well: She never hesitated to trust in his goodness and to rest in his embrace. She believed we can never have too much confidence in our gracious God, who is powerful and merciful. We obtain from him as much as we hope for.

The lordship of Jesus, Thérèse believed, is one of love. He is not a tyrannical despot who selfishly hoards the riches of his kingdom. Rather he wants to lavish gifts and graces on the beloved children of his Father, the heirs of the kingdom of God.

The fundamental reason for Thérèse's confidence was her belief that Jesus loves us all infinitely. He demonstrated the greatest love possible in suffering and dying for each of us. How could she doubt the goodness and promises of such a friend and savior? "Your love reaches unto folly," she wrote. "In the presence of this folly, how can You not desire that my heart leap toward You? How can my confidence, then, have any limits?"[11]

In the Sermon on the Mount, Jesus teaches that the poor in spirit are blessed because theirs is the kingdom of heaven. Saint Thérèse's teachings on littleness help us understand what it means to have this poverty of spirit. Those who do not claim to be spiritually rich, who humbly recognize their poverty and their littleness, have a place in the kingdom of God. God can share his life with those whose lives aren't already spoken for. He can bestow his blessings on those who are ready to receive them. We may be infinitely poor in comparison to God, but that means we simply must receive everything from God.

This confidence in Christ's goodness enabled Thérèse to make bold requests of God. She didn't fear to ask *everything* of him. And not only did she ask, but she always expected God to answer her every request.

Thérèse was especially confident when it came to seeking things she knew Jesus wanted to give her. She fully trusted that he would do in her what she could not do on her own. She believed that Jesus intended to help her in every way. After all, he *commanded* us to love him with our whole heart, mind, and soul. She rejoiced in this commandment, exclaiming, "Oh, how good it is that God has commanded us to love Him. Otherwise we would never have dared to."[12]

A New Heart

Poverty of spirit paves the way for sanctity—for the kingdom of God within us. Thérèse wrote, "God alone, content with my weak efforts, will raise me to Himself and make me a *saint*, clothing me in His infinite merits."[13] She believed she was poor even in her love for the Lord, but she knew that his love would make up for the poverty of her heart. She made the prayer of the psalmist her own: "Create in me a clean heart, O God" (Psalm 51:10).

But Thérèse didn't stop at asking God for a new heart. She knew Jesus commanded her to nourish a love that went beyond natural human love when he commanded us to "love one another as I have loved you" (John 15:12). So Thérèse begged Jesus to give her his own heart, his divine heart, his sacred heart burning with perfect, infinite charity. "To love You as You love me, I would have to borrow Your own Love, and then only would I be at rest,"[14] she prayed to Jesus. How could she go wrong if her heart was joined to the very heart of Christ?

Saint Thérèse asked Jesus to draw her into the flames of his love, to unite her so intimately to him that he would truly live and act in her. She longed to say with Saint Paul, "It is no longer I who live, but Christ who lives in me" (Galatians 2:20).

But can it be so simple "merely to take Jesus by His Heart"?[15] Thérèse believed it was. She confidently made this request, in such beautiful words as these:

> Ah! Give me a thousand hearts to love you.
> But that is still too little, Jesus, Beauty Supreme.
> Give me your divine Heart itself to love you….
>
> …It's your love that has to transform me.
> Put in my heart your consuming flame,

And I'll be able to bless you and love you.[16]

O my divine Savior, I rest upon your heart. It is mine![17]

Saint Thérèse teaches us that we need the love of Jesus to fill our hearts if we hope to love God as we should. This is an essential insight in our quest to love God with our whole heart.

LIVING THE LESSONS

Saint Thérèse of Lisieux loved God with heartfelt passion. Her love for him was a profound experience that often left her reeling in the attempt to convey the infinite beauty of her Beloved. "I feel how powerless I am to express in human language the secrets of heaven.... There are so many different horizons, so many nuances of infinite variety that only the palette of the Celestial Painter will be able to furnish me…with the colors capable of depicting the marvels He reveals."[18]

Our goal is to love God so much that we feel for him what Saint Thérèse felt in the depths of her heart. But in learning about Thérèse—about her great love, her humble Little Way, her trust in Jesus—we may face doubts and concerns. She was one of those few souls who never committed serious sin; few of us can claim such a history. So how does her journey relate to us? Can we really have the love and confidence Thérèse had? With our past sins and current struggles, can we still fill our hearts with love for God? Thérèse said that we can.

Letting God Lead

Thérèse loved the example of Mary Magdalene, who though she had been a sinner, accepted Christ's forgiveness with love and confidence. Whenever Thérèse pondered the depth of mercy Mary Magdalene experienced, all fear and doubt left her heart.

In the last days of her life she said, "It is not because I have been preserved from mortal sin that I raise my heart to God in trust and love. Ah! I feel that if I had every imaginable crime on my conscience I should still not lose my confidence; with my heart broken by repentance I should throw myself into the arms of my Saviour."[19]

Thérèse understood that Jesus gives his love freely. We only need to be humble enough to receive it. Confidence in Christ is all we need to make that essential prayer, asking for Jesus' own heart, his own love to fill us so we can love God as he deserves to be loved.

This self-abandonment can be difficult. We sometimes imagine ourselves bigger and more powerful than we are, and so we resist the help of the "Eagle." We try to do things on our own. But that leads to trouble.

Thérèse expresses this well in a reflection about Saint Peter. She felt sure that if Saint Peter had humbly asked Jesus for the grace to follow him even unto death, he would have received that grace immediately. But Peter didn't ask for that grace. Instead he boldly professed his own strength and commitment. And then he fell: He denied his Lord. Thérèse believed that if Peter had acknowledged his littleness before Christ, things would have turned out differently.

We can accomplish much more when we stop relying on our own power and let God work through us. This doesn't mean we are to become passive or idle, however; Thérèse was well aware of that. She saw her life as an opportunity to actively express her love for Jesus.

Actions as Offerings

Even though she knew her actions could never buy his love,

Thérèse still longed to offer *something* to her beloved Jesus. She didn't presume to offer anything extraordinary; she knew her limitations. Instead of attempting to impress Jesus with marvelous works, she decided to shower him with small tokens of her love. She often spoke of gathering little flowers of sacrifice and devotion and offering them to Jesus for his pleasure. As she said, "[T]here's only one thing to do here below—strew before Jesus the flowers of little sacrifices, and win Him with caresses."[20]

Thérèse wanted to perfume the royal throne with the sweet scents of these "flowers." "Let us make our heart a little garden of delight where Jesus may come to find rest,"[21] she said. She wanted to do little things out of love to charm the heart of Christ. When she wanted to scowl, she smiled. When she wanted to complain, she praised. When she wanted to be lazy, she worked.

We can offer these same tokens to Christ. We can hold back a bitter reply when we're tempted to get verbal revenge. Perhaps a coworker makes an unfounded accusation, or a family member offers unsolicited advice. These are opportunities to practice self-control and charity, opportunities to give a little gift to Jesus.

We can also look for opportunities to serve others without recognition. Thérèse loved the amusing challenge of finding ways to do good deeds anonymously. She took the worst spot during laundry duty. She gave the last swig of apple cider to the thirsty sister sitting next to her. She smiled without fail at the most vexing nun in the convent. She showed her love for Jesus every day in minutiae like this.

These "little" actions can be the stuff of sainthood. Sanctity doesn't require anything other than a heart full of love. Thérèse knew everyone could become holy, so she cried out, "Believe me, don't wait until tomorrow to begin becoming a saint!"[22]

Scared to be a Saint?

Learning that sanctity is within our reach poses a personal challenge to each of us. What will we try to change? What will we need to give up? Maintaining the false notion that sainthood is for someone with a more exotic situation, a cleaner past, or a bigger heart allows us to stay comfortably dormant. But Thérèse shows us that our lives are sufficient, that God's mercy can heal our past, and that he can refashion our hearts.

From her youth Thérèse loved Jesus with her whole heart, and she never regretted it. In addition to bringing her personal consolation, this love helped her grow in her relationships with others. She understood that when we give ourselves to God, our hearts don't lose their natural tenderness; rather that tenderness increases as our hearts become purer and more divine. Thérèse wrote, "[I]n loving Him the heart expands and can give to those who are dear to it incomparably more tenderness than if it had concentrated upon one egotistical and unfruitful love."[23]

Loving God enriches not only our experience of human love but also our experience of life. Thérèse was able to see the gifts of her Beloved surrounding her. She was passionately engaged in life. She loved to explore nature and absorb the beauties of creation. She loved to celebrate Church festivals: "The *feasts!*... How I loved the *feasts!*"[24] The love overflowing from her heart spilled out in her many poems and plays. Her love for God energized her daily life. She lived as a woman in love: joyful, enthusiastic, smiling.

Even in the face of the immense difficulties of her life, Thérèse never lashed out at Jesus. She didn't forsake his love in the tough times. She accepted everything with grace and resigned herself to God's will. During her greatest physical suffering at the end of her life, people asked her if she was hoping for a quick death to end her misery. Thérèse always responded that whether she lived or died didn't matter to her. She was honestly content to live or die according to the will of God.

Love like this is beyond our normal human strength, but God desires to give it to us. That's why he can ask us to love him with complete surrender and willingness. As Thérèse once said, "How much the divine teachings run contrary to our natural feelings. Without the aid of grace it would be impossible even to understand them, let alone to practise them."[25]

We need grace to love God the way he deserves to be loved. This grace comes into our hearts when we ask Jesus to share his heart with us.

Remembering Saint Thérèse's promise to continue her work from heaven, let us ask for her intercession. The Doctor of Spiritual Childhood continues to offer her devotees little tokens of affection, strewing flowers of answered prayers. Indeed, we can be confident that Thérèse will intercede for us as we seek to love God wholeheartedly and to join her one day in the eternal embrace of the one Love that satisfies the deepest longings of every human heart.

For Reflection

- Which of Saint Thérèse's qualities do I most admire?
- How could these qualities become part of who I am?

Ten Ways to Be More Like Saint Thérèse of Lisieux

1. Make an act of consecration to Mary.
2. Look for God in nature.
3. Read *The Imitation of Christ* by Thomas à Kempis.
4. Write letters to friends and family about your love for Jesus.
5. Pray earnestly for priests.
6. Keep a journal of your spiritual life.
7. Foster a devotion to the Sacred Heart of Jesus.
8. Spend time with children.
9. Make at least one sacrifice every day without being noticed.
10. Express your relationship with Jesus through poetry or artwork.

Points for Consideration

• Saint Thérèse saw God in nature, but she didn't see nature as God. When she beheld the beauty of creation, she remembered the Creator. This protected her from allowing anything or anyone, other than God himself, to capture her heart. She knew that the beauties, joys, and pleasures of the earth are gifts from God, not substitutes for him.
Consider: What created things might threaten to become substitutes for God in my life?

• Within convent walls Saint Thérèse found contentment. She embraced her surroundings and noticed the joys present there. She took advantage of every opportunity to make her daily life an adventure, finding opportunities to rejoice, to love, and to grow.
Consider: Do I notice and celebrate the joys of nature, family, friendship, and faith in my daily life?

- Imperfection is part of being human, and Saint Thérèse knew it. She saw her weaknesses clearly. She claimed them as her own without making excuses or letting them depress or overwhelm her. She chose to be encouraged instead of discouraged. She believed that humbly acknowledging her inability to be perfect was an invitation to let God work.

  Consider: How can I overcome any discouragement about my weaknesses?

- Like us, Saint Thérèse lived, worked, and prayed among people she liked and people she didn't like. She approached her relationships, especially the trying ones, as opportunities to express her love for God. She saw each frustrating situation as a gift, because it enabled her to offer a little sacrifice to the Lord.

  Consider: What difficult relationships in my life give me opportunities to offer loving sacrifices to God?

- Saint Thérèse wasn't afraid to ask for anything. She didn't hold back from asking for little gifts from her father or from making her request of the pope. Neither did she refrain from asking favors of Jesus every day. Her life was full of answered prayers because she wasn't afraid to ask.

  Consider: What special request can I bring to Jesus?

chapter two

❋ SAINT TERESA OF AVILA ❋
Loving God With Your Whole Soul

*Examine yourselves, to see whether you are holding to your
faith.... Do you not realize that Jesus Christ is in you?*
2 Corinthians 13:5

HER LIFE

Teresa Sanchez de Cepeda y Ahumada's life began in Avila,
Spain, at 5:30 AM on March 28, 1515. Her father, Don Alonso,
said she came "with the first glimmers of the light of day."[1] This
was perfect timing for a woman who would be a bright light in
a struggling Church during the Protestant Reformation and the
Spanish Inquisition.

Teresa's mother was Don Alonso's second wife. Along with
a half-brother and-half sister, Teresa had six other brothers and
one sister, born to the feeble Doña Beatriz, who died when
Teresa was only thirteen years old. Rodrigo, the closest brother
in age to Teresa, was her dearest companion. The young pair
frequently collaborated on secret plans whose innocent designs
often revolved around experiencing the glories of martyrdom.

Teresa did not expend all her social efforts on her brother,
however. Many people were attracted to her, and not just because
of her good looks. She had an unusually large share of charms
that she enjoyed displaying for others. (She later described them
as the natural graces with which the Lord had endowed her.) She

was clever, witty, and gifted in writing, dance, embroidery, chess, and horseback riding.

The people of Avila were of the opinion that Teresa would marry whomever she pleased. And indeed she did, although the journey that led her to be the bride of Christ was not a direct one.

In her autobiography Saint Teresa shares a candid confession of the sins and weaknesses she struggled with throughout her life. She reveals how eagerly she sought the approval of people around her by dressing according to fashion, wearing jewelry and makeup as soon as she could, and being almost fixated on her appearance. Along with her vain tendencies, as a girl she was addicted to reading books of chivalry and following the lives of their characters. Her father didn't approve of this pastime, but she would disobey him by reading them in secret.

Teresa also had a tendency to foster exclusive friendships whose primary sustenance was gossip. Instead of following her older sister's example of modesty and charity, Teresa latched on to her cousin, who was not a good influence in this regard. (Later Teresa would teach that we are more inclined to follow bad examples than good ones.)

Leaving behind the effects of these adolescent tendencies was a difficult challenge for Teresa. But at the age of sixteen, she went to a girls' boarding school run by sisters of the Augustinian order, and there she began to grow in her knowledge of God. She also started fighting some of her sinful habits, mostly because she was afraid of eternal punishment.

Teresa was not yet acting out of love for Jesus. She says honestly of her teenage years, "I was still most anxious not to be a nun."[2] Five more years would pass before God gave her the desire to enter religious life.

A Vocation in the Making

In the meantime Teresa fell ill. The sickness progressed to the point where she had to leave school and move back into her father's house. There she spent many days confined to her bed. As she began to feel better, she decided she would prefer a different setting. So while still convalescing, Teresa moved in with her older sister Maria, who was married and had a young son.

Teresa enjoyed herself immensely in her new home, playing with her nephew and improving her already noteworthy cooking skills. The experience of staying with her sister, however, did not leave Teresa with a longing for married life. In fact, her choice to join the convent was largely made during this time. She also visited her uncle, whose deep faith and spiritual conversation influenced her.

Teresa did not feel an *emotional* attraction to being a nun. But the thoughts she began to have about the vanity of the world and the horror of hell led her to make a deliberate choice to remove herself from the temptations to her particular weaknesses. As she recalled, "I decided to make myself enter."[3]

By the time she was twenty-one, Teresa was ready to carry out her plan. Leaving her family was a tremendous sacrifice, which she only managed through the strength of her resolution. And so she became the Carmelite Sister Teresa of Jesus. Although it began only as an act of her will, entering the Carmelite order would bring Teresa a deep joy that lasted throughout her whole life.

Her joy was not without suffering, however. Teresa soon became ill again, and this sickness affected her more dramatically than the previous one. She had to leave her new convent home and seek treatment elsewhere. The doctors' methods were often torturous, and Teresa's health only worsened in their hands.

At one point Teresa asked to receive the last rites, but when the priest arrived, he thought she was dead. The next two days she showed no sign of life. The following day the nuns prepared a grave for her and wrapped her body in a shroud. On the fourth day the sisters came to take her body, but Teresa's father resisted, believing she was still alive. Sure enough, Teresa opened her eyes and immediately asked if she could make a confession and receive the Eucharist.

Teresa was slow to recover from this physical trauma. She returned to her father's home, completely paralyzed except for movement in one finger on her right hand. She was in excruciating pain for nine months.

Finally Teresa returned to her Carmelite convent, where she lived in the infirmary for three years. She kept up her spirits with the attitude that she would not exchange her suffering for any treasure. She believed suffering was a gift from God to draw her closer to him. She accepted his will for her, even if it would mean being in this state forever. The other sisters marveled at her patience during this time of trial, because it seemed impossible, were it not for God's grace, that anyone could bear so much with such great joy.

Eventually Teresa began to pray through the intercession of Saint Joseph that God would cure her so she could serve him. Shortly thereafter she showed remarkable improvement, and before long she was participating once again in normal life at the convent. But as Teresa was soon to discover, life in the convent was in some ways too normal.

A Carmelite Conversion
Over time the Carmelite nuns had become lax in the observance of their rule. In place of poverty and austerity, luxury had crept

in. Some of the wealthier nuns had cells that resembled small mansions, complete with fashionable furnishings and servants. The community had also abandoned many traditional practices of silence and fasting in favor of a more comfortable way of life.

Perhaps the greatest problem for Teresa was that the Carmel served as a popular social center for many people, including wealthy and noble personages of the surrounding area. The sisters (especially Teresa, who was quite popular) would spend hours gossiping with guests rather than conversing with Christ. With this company Teresa kept one foot in the secular world. She even gave up her prayer life for a time, until her father was dying and his confessor urged Teresa to return to prayer. It would be another ten years before Teresa was ready to give herself entirely to Jesus.

During a festival the sisters celebrated in their house, Teresa began to desire to truly love Jesus and never to offend him through sin. For this feast the sisters had on loan a special statue of Christ for their chapel. (In the sixteenth century sacred works of art couldn't be mass-produced and distributed, so the arrival of this sculpture was significant.) The image portrayed Christ with the wounds of his passion. Teresa wrote: "[T]he very sight of Him shook me, for it clearly showed what He suffered for us. So strongly did I feel what a poor return I had made for those wounds, that my heart seemed to break, and I threw myself on the ground before Him in a great flood of tears, imploring Him to give me strength once and for all not to offend Him again."[4]

This was a moment of profound conversion in Saint Teresa's life. She began to recognize the truth about sin, and this helped prepare her soul for the grace of complete mystical union with Jesus. She progressed steadily in her spiritual life and in prayer from this point forward.

Along with all her soul's growth in the ensuing years, Saint Teresa was also busy with another massive undertaking: the reform of the Carmelite order. Seven years after her conversion experience, on a Saturday evening in her cell (which was large and comfortable enough to entertain guests), Teresa was talking with some of her close companions when the idea came up to found a new convent, more sincerely dedicated to the pursuit of holiness and perfection. In the following days Teresa felt God calling her to pursue this new convent and to name it in honor of Saint Joseph.

Teresa's biggest hesitation, superficial though it may have been, was that she liked the house where she was because she had arranged her cell exactly to her taste. Resisting this temptation to take the easy route, she decided to implement reforms that would be more conducive to the advancement of souls in the ways of prayer. She thus began her work of founding the reformed branch of the Carmelite order, the Discalced Carmelites. *Discalced*, which means "shoeless," indicates the return to the austere roots of Carmelite life.

Before pursuing plans for the new convent of Saint Joseph, Teresa sought approval from her confessor and the Carmelite provincial, both of whom supported her plan at first. But when certain sisters in Teresa's community and members of some other orders showed resistance, these men changed their minds. Teresa faced the scorn and judgment of many who disapproved of the changes.

Teresa endured this opposition courageously, finally opening the new convent two years later. In the remaining twenty years of her life, she would help establish fifteen other Discalced Carmelite convents, including the community of Discalced Brothers, which Saint John of the Cross founded with her.

Teresa maintained many contacts in these years, during which she wrote her *Book of Foundations*. She sent letters and paid visits to priories and palaces, nobles, priests, and bishops. Some people accused her of vanity and pride, of making herself out to be more important than she was. But fame and attention did not motivate Teresa; she actually wished she had less of it. In the chapel, for example, when she felt she was about to enter into a state of ecstasy, she begged God to spare her from any public display. She was afraid others might mistakenly think she was worthy of these special graces.

Teresa had no desire to be set apart as "the holy one," because she believed she was far from perfect. She told a priest, "[D]uring my lifetime, I have been told that I was handsome and I believed it; that I was clever and I thought it was true; and that I was a Saint, but I always knew that people were mistaken on that score."[5]

Teresa's reputation for sanctity spread, in spite of her protests, among those who weren't blinded by jealousy. Try as she might to bring her flaws to light, the Light of Christ shone more brightly within her. This holy radiance shone around her and all the saints because they carried Jesus within them. Saint Teresa's life of prayer made this divine presence possible.

Her Lessons

Saint Teresa's great love for Jesus began to flourish when she developed an authentic prayer life. She claims that she didn't begin to pray until years after she had become a Carmelite nun. But surely she had long been "praying" the rosary and the Liturgy of the Hours and praying at daily Mass. What did she mean by saying she had the love of God "ever since I began to pray"?[6]

Meeting Jesus in Prayer

According to Saint Teresa—one of the Church's great spiritual masters—prayer is a matter of coming into living contact with Jesus; it is not just recitation and repetition. Simply going through the motions doesn't deserve the noble title of "prayer," and it won't lead to the union of our souls with Jesus. It was only through her living contact with Jesus that Saint Teresa began to love him.

Before she started praying with sincerity and devotion, Saint Teresa was typically preoccupied with waiting for her allotted prayer time to end and listening for the striking of the clock. (This is reassuring for those of us who find that prayer challenges our attention spans.) Saint Teresa actually spent more than eighteen years struggling in her prayer, pulled between conversing with God and being caught up in the activities of the world.

But eventually she recognized the need to focus on whom we are praying to with our minds, not just our mouths. In *Interior Castle* she wrote, "If a person does not think [of] Whom he is addressing, and what he is asking for, and who it is that is asking and of Whom he is asking it, I do not consider that he is praying at all even though he be constantly moving his lips."[7] And in the book she wrote especially for the young sisters of her order, *The Way of Perfection*, she begs them not to address God while they are thinking of other things.[8]

Teresa also compares a person's relationship to Jesus with a woman's relationship to her husband. A good wife knows her husband. She understands him, cares for him, and is attentive to him. When he speaks to her, she listens. And when she speaks to him, she knows the person she's talking to. Because of their personal knowledge, their conversations have the potential to be more than just empty exchanges of words. Similarly, if a soul knows Jesus, understands him, cares about him, and is attentive to him, prayer can be truly meaningful. At the root of prayer is a relationship of love.

Saint Teresa warns against reciting the Our Father or attending Mass without thinking about the encounter with Christ. Staying focused in prayer requires effort and discipline; it's often easier to daydream. But the soul will begin to experience the presence of Jesus in a deeper way when it engages him directly.

Saint Teresa refers to the early stages of prayer as "frequent solitary conversation with Him who, as we know, loves us."[9] Tasting the sweetness of loving conversation with Jesus, even in its simplest form, makes the soul yearn for more. However, this doesn't imply that prayer will always be easy. Saint Teresa refers to the four stages of prayer in terms of "the four methods of watering."[10]

The soul's effort to unite with Jesus in prayer is sometimes like drawing water from a well: It involves a lot of muscle power and labor. At other times, by God's grace, the efforts are less difficult, like collecting water from a water wheel. Occasionally a soul will be able to simply draw water from a "river" that God provides in his goodness. And if God sees fit, he can even send a heavenly spiritual rain that requires no action from the soul.

Since God's wisdom and timing—not our power—bring the heavenly showers, we are to simply focus on that which *is* in our power. We draw water from the "well" by staying dedicated to our prayer time and keeping our attention focused, until God should lead us somewhere else. But even this stage, with all its effort, can be a joy because it is an expression of love for Jesus.

The stronger this loving relationship becomes, the more perfectly united the soul is to Jesus.

Saint Teresa's prayer life did culminate in the "spiritual rain" of mystical union with Christ. Evidence of her celestial transports is present throughout her writings. She sometimes interrupted everything to converse with Jesus in the eloquent language of prayer. Yet she remained remarkably down-to-earth for a woman who experienced divine rapture on a regular basis.

At her more advanced stages of spiritual life, Teresa's union with Jesus was so profound that she was aware of his presence in her soul every minute. This is why she thought nothing of pausing to speak with him every now and again. By sharing these intimate moments in her writings, Saint Teresa has left us a beautiful testimony to the fruits of loving Jesus with the whole soul.

The Significance of the Soul

In *Interior Castle* Saint Teresa describes the union of the soul with Christ and the journey leading up to this spiritual pinnacle. This doctor of the Church captures the nuances of one of the most indescribable human experiences. Although she struggled to perfectly express the grandeur of the soul's union with Jesus, Saint Teresa still offered beautiful descriptions: "[It is] so sublime a favour, and such delight is felt by the soul, that I do not know with what to compare it, beyond saying that the Lord is pleased to manifest to the soul at that moment the glory that is in Heaven."[11]

Saint Teresa shares about her experience of complete unity with Jesus, but she never claims to deserve these graces. She wrote not to boast but to help other souls love Jesus and experience this spiritual connection with him. Her readers find practical advice on how to approach this union, from a woman who knew that the intimacy she experienced was not something she had merited or deserved. Anyone can be a recipient of this grace in the soul. Teresa knew this because she knew the tremendous dignity of every human soul.

God inspired Saint Teresa with profound insights into the nature of the human soul. Faced with the writing assignment—given by her superior—that was destined to be her masterpiece, Saint Teresa began *Interior Castle* with an exasperated prayer. She asked God to speak through her, since she couldn't think of anything to say and had no clue where to start. Through the inspiration of this prayer, she came up with one of her most famous analogies:

> I began to think of the soul as if it were a castle made of a single diamond or of very clear crystal, in which there are many rooms, just as in Heaven there are many mansions [see John 14:2]. Now if we think carefully over this, sisters, the soul of the righteous man is nothing but a paradise, in which, as God tells us, He takes His delight....
>
> ...[I]n the centre and midst of them all is the chiefest mansion where the most secret things pass between God and the soul....
>
> [I]f this castle is the soul, there can clearly be no question of our entering it. For we ourselves are the castle.[12]

This analogy encourages us to recognize our soul as something beautiful, as a place where God takes delight. He loves us enough to want to dwell in the depths of our being. He desires to be as close to us as we are to ourselves. This realization made

Saint Teresa long to transform her soul into a fitting place for the presence of God himself.

Saint Teresa also speaks philosophically about the soul. She often refers to the faculties of the soul: the intellect, the will, the imagination, and the memory. As she describes the various stages of prayer that she experienced, she explains how they affected each faculty of the soul. Except for the most sublime experiences of union, Saint Teresa's soul was not *completely* united to God because the faculties weren't all behaving.

"My will, I believe, is good," she wrote. "But this intellect of mine is so wild that it seems like a raving lunatic. Nobody can hold it down, and I have not sufficient control over it myself to keep it quiet for a single moment."[13] But Saint Teresa persevered in prayer even when she experienced such distraction.

Throughout her writings Saint Teresa employs the word *soul* almost interchangeably with *self*. "When a soul has reached this point,"[14] she might write in reference to a person who prays well, or, "This soul longs to be free,"[15] she might declare of the longing she felt in her whole being for union with God. Saint Teresa believed the soul was the core of human identity. For her, loving God with the whole soul meant loving with the whole self, the whole being, everything one has to give.

According to Teresa's analogy, there are many rooms in the castle of our soul where this love is meant to bloom. We move through the outer rooms before we arrive at the innermost chamber. This movement is part of the process of growing in love. The most interior room represents the closest union with Jesus any soul can have this side of heaven, the fullness of the spiritual life. Saint Teresa described this great unity between Christ and the soul as the spiritual marriage.

As we move from the outermost rooms to the inner rooms of our soul-castle, we proceed along the path that prepares us for the deepest, most unitive prayer, where Jesus wraps our whole soul in his love. But the journey doesn't happen automatically. Saint Teresa arrived at this point after many years and much effort. And when she did, the love of God consumed her soul.

In one of her transports of ecstasy, Teresa wrote: "[A]s I write this I am still under the power of that heavenly madness, the effect of Your goodness and mercy, O my King. . . . [I] can no longer suffer such trials as come when [I am] without You. . . . [N]othing can comfort [me] now but You."[16] She progressed to such unity with God that she longed for nothing more than his presence within her.

We have the advantage of learning from Teresa's wisdom and experience. As we seek to love God with our whole soul, she teaches us the importance of three things: 1) overcoming sin, 2) developing virtue, and 3) offering our entire will to God.

Overcoming Sin

Returning to the image of our souls as beautiful crystal castles, the question arises: How much have we done to keep the crystal clear? Have we made our souls beautiful mansions for God, or have we allowed our souls to become dank and dingy? When we remember that we are hosting an honored Guest, we're more likely to keep our souls clean, to repent of sin and strive for holiness.

Sometimes we imagine that the saints easily conquered sin. But more often than not, they, too, had to work diligently to recognize and eliminate sinful behavior. Saint Teresa was no exception. She spent years becoming aware of her own failings and striving to overcome them. She recalls,

[I]t was some time before I came to see it. I knew perfectly well that I had a soul, but I did not understand what that soul merited, or Who dwelt within it.... I think, if I had understood then, as I do now, how this great King *really* dwells within this little palace of my soul, I should not have left Him alone so often, but should have stayed with Him and never have allowed His dwelling-place to get so dirty.[17]

The question of sin is really a question of love. Saint Teresa assures us that if we resist sin out of love for God, he can make a magnificent dwelling in our soul. This requires effort and sacrifice, working diligently to recognize our sins and praying for grace to overcome them. It involves striving to give up our sins even while we are still attached to them.

Saint Teresa speaks about the attachments to worldly vanity that she had so much trouble overcoming. Becoming holy takes perseverance and dedication. But Teresa helps motivate us. Speaking of the union of the soul with God, she says, "On arriving at this state, the soul...clearly sees that...there are no riches, estates, honours, or delights that can give it such satisfaction even for the twinkling of an eye. For this is the true joy, the content that can be seen to satisfy."[18]

Developing Virtue

Working to overcome sin is the first step to uniting our souls to God. But true love is not satisfied with simply overcoming problems. True love goes further, offering "unnecessary" expressions of devotion. We want to do more than just avoid evil: We want to cultivate goodness.

Saint Teresa knew that developing virtue was part of truly loving Jesus. She presents the image of the virtues as beautiful adornments that make our interior castle a fit dwelling place for the King. She believed that two of the greatest virtues are detachment and humility.

Developing detachment. By detachment Saint Teresa means freedom from craving worldly things. This virtue frees us to pursue the truly important and fulfilling things in life.

Saint Teresa had an insight into this virtue when she ventured away from the convent to visit a prominent and wealthy woman. While staying at the home of this noble lady, Teresa was able to see all of the constraints that constantly burdened such a life. Always dressing, eating, and socializing according to her noble rank made this woman little more than a slave. The distractions of this worldly existence made Saint Teresa long to return to the simplicity that allowed her to focus on Jesus.

Saint Teresa recognized the great irony that the masters of the world are often slaves to pomp and circumstance. The virtue of detachment frees us from this slavery. Saint Teresa assures us that when we stay focused on our true Master, our cravings for these limited delights will begin to disappear.

Deep down, Teresa assures us, we know it is a mistake to think that these fleeting, earthly things can compete with being united to God. In the end what good are honors, pleasures, and successes if they detract from our relationship with God? When we choose these worldly things over him, we are not fully loving him. Detachment frees us to love the way we are called to love, foreign though it may be in the eyes of the world. Even Saint Teresa referred to her love of Jesus as "heavenly madness."[19]

Yet Teresa struggled during the course of her life to overcome selfish attachments, particularly her desire for the approval of others and the pleasures of being popular. Humility was an essential virtue in this task: In fact, she came to believe that this was the most important virtue in the spiritual life.

Growing in humility. A disclaimer begins Saint Teresa's autobiography. She states that if her confessor (who instructed her to write the book) had allowed it, she would have spent her time reporting on her sins and faults. She begs her readers to bear in mind her many failings as they read about the favors the Lord granted her. This humility is Saint Teresa's fundamental attitude throughout the book. She recognizes her own weaknesses, which make her all the more grateful for the gifts and graces God gave her.

Saint Teresa's genuine expressions of humility are woven throughout her stories and her teachings. We also learn by observing her example. She was quick to admit fault and slow to accuse anyone else. She constantly gave thanks for the benefits she received, never expecting or demanding them. She paid tribute to those who were wiser and holier than her, always seeking guidance and advice instead of presuming on her own knowledge or insights. And all this from a woman who experienced raptures, ecstasies, and visions, who became a doctor of the Church, and who was destined to be one of the most popular mystical writers in all of history.

This great saint knew God's infinite goodness in such an intimate way that she was keenly aware of her finite limitations. She had a deep awareness of the free gifts God had given her, gifts she could never earn. Her humility stemmed from her profound understanding of the mercy and goodness of God.

It is fitting that Saint Teresa never claimed to be an example of humility. But she did write directly about the importance of the virtue. She believed that all the other virtues, and indeed the whole spiritual life, depend upon humility, because it grounds us in reality. She wrote, "To be humble is to walk in truth."[20] Humility keeps us from any false notions about ourselves or about God.

Humility is the antidote to the sin of pride, which denies our complete dependence on God. Humility does not mean downplaying our gifts or talents in order to avoid boasting. Neither does humility produce weak people who cannot assert themselves. (These are common misconceptions.) Authentically humble people simply know who they are because they know how they relate to God.

Saint Teresa felt we could never succeed in knowing ourselves unless we were seeking to know God. He is our Creator, so our very existence is a gift from him. He sustains our life, and he knows us better than we know ourselves. Acknowledging this means we realize our complete dependence on God (we wouldn't be here if it wasn't for him), our selfish tendencies (compared to the selfless love of God, who sent his Son to die for us), and our powerlessness (God is all-powerful, and we are not). Knowledge of God is also reassuring because we know God created us out of love. This love gives us the confidence to trust in his power over our lives.

Saint Teresa believed that humility would never disquiet, trouble, or disturb the soul; rather peace, joy, and tranquility always accompany this virtue. When this peace is present in the soul, it is not difficult to trust in God. Knowing his goodness and power is comforting once we acknowledge our own limits. With this humble trust in God, we can freely and confidently surrender our lives to his loving care.

Offering Her Will to God

Surrender to God was an essential element in preparing Saint Teresa for her soul's union with him. She frequently pointed out that any union a soul has with God comes through divine initiative. The Lord is free to unite himself to a soul that has not followed the specific guidelines she presents. But she encourages us to continue to draw water from the well diligently rather than wait for a rainfall from heaven. Giving our wills to God prepares the climate of our souls. And the rains are much more likely to come when the climate is right.

Saint Teresa knew it would be a mistake not to resign herself completely to what the Lord was doing in her life, because he knows exactly what suits each of us. Our vision is limited: It is often difficult for us to put our lives into the big picture of God's will for us. We sometimes fight God when troubles arise, presuming that we know better than he does. It's much more fruitful to humbly accept what is happening, trusting that God knows what he's doing even if we don't.

God gave us his Son, who gave us the perfect example of complete, loving surrender to the Father when he prayed, "Not my will, but yours be done" (Luke 22:42). We make the same prayer every time we say the Our Father. Saint Teresa encourages us to pray these words honestly. When we say, "Thy kingdom come, Thy will be done," we are offering *our* will to God.

Love is at the root of our surrender. Jesus loved us enough to die for us, and he gave everything to be in a loving relationship with us. But he will not force us to love him in return: That would not be love. Instead he invites us to love him and awaits our response. He does not manipulate or pressure us: We decide whether or not we will say yes to his invitation.

LIVING THE LESSONS

The choice to give our soul completely to God, as Saint Teresa did, can seem deceptively simple: "God wants your soul to experience heavenly bliss, now and for all eternity. Would you like to accept or decline?" Accept, of course! But an honest consideration ought to follow Saint Teresa's lessons on the union of the soul with Christ. The love she bore in her soul did not mature overnight. It came through her conversion and a corresponding commitment to the commandments.

By dying on the cross for us, Jesus freed us from our sins. Truly accepting this gift of freedom can't help but have an effect on our lives. Thinking of the love Jesus has shown us on the cross helps us to love him in return. Remember the image of the wounded Christ that had such an impact on Saint Teresa? If we want to experience a similar conversion in our lives, we can follow her advice to always fix our eyes on our crucified Savior. When we do, keeping the commandments becomes easier and easier. We see them as gifts that God gave us to help prepare our souls to welcome him.

On the other hand, when we are not seeking a loving relationship with God, we want to be "free" to act selfishly. Rooting out that selfishness is a necessary first step to loving God. This helps us seek a different freedom: the freedom from any threat of sin, the freedom to love God as he deserves to be loved.

We can follow Teresa's example of loving God through the generous offering of self-surrender. We can also make our souls fertile ground for a rich spiritual harvest by striving to overcome sin and develop virtue. Working against any barriers to God's love and readying ourselves to welcome him prepares us to be fully united with him.

Surrender to the Master of our soul is not just a proclamation or a good intention. This surrender, if it is complete, will also affect our actions. It includes the ordering of our lives as God directs.

But why would we give up our "freedom" and promise to order our lives according to someone else's will? Because God is all-knowing, all-loving, and all-powerful. He knows what's best for us, desires our true happiness, and can arrange everything for our benefit.

As we wrap up this chapter full of challenges, remember that Saint Teresa didn't start out too differently from most of us. She had to overcome sin, selfishness, and vanity. But she took great consolation in the fact that many saints before her had to do the same. She commended herself to various saints at different points in her life, including Saint Mary Magdalene and Saint Augustine.

Saint Teresa had a particular affection for Saint Augustine, whose conversion story was a favorite of hers. When she read his *Confessions,* she saw herself portrayed there. Saint Augustine's change of heart made her feel as if God had spoken directly to her. This is often the effect when we read about the saints: God speaks to us through them. Indeed, he calls us to join their company!

Saint Teresa once told her sisters, "God deliver us, sisters, from saying 'We are not angels,' or 'We are not saints,' whenever we commit some imperfection. We may not be; but what a good thing it is for us to reflect that we can be if we will only try and if God gives us His hand!"[21]

God's grace can transform us into saints. Our job is to surrender ourselves to this action in our souls. This surrender is the beginning of our soul's union with God, in which we "abandon" ourselves "into the arms of love,"[22] as Saint Teresa wrote. What rejoicing we will feel in the depths of our being when we can exclaim with Saint Teresa, "O Jesus my Lord, how precious Your love is!"[23]

FOR REFLECTION

- Which of Saint Teresa's qualities do I most admire?
- How could these qualities become part of who I am?

TEN WAYS TO BE MORE LIKE SAINT TERESA OF AVILA

1. Meditate on a passage from the Gospels.
2. Keep silent when you are falsely accused, unless it would cause scandal.
3. Meet regularly with a good spiritual director.
4. Ask God to reveal how you can use your gifts to serve the Church.
5. Do acts of penance, even outside of Lent.
6. Examine your conscience whenever you glance in a mirror.
7. Participate in a program that helps form young people in their faith.
8. Go to confession monthly.
9. Redirect gossip by publicly giving the benefit of the doubt to the victim.
10. Attend daily Mass more often than you go shopping.

POINTS FOR CONSIDERATION

- If the young Teresa were alive today, she might be inclined to read *Vogue, Glamour, In Style,* and *People* magazines and to gossip with her friends. Like many of us, she had to battle to free herself from her intense desire to have a perfect appearance and to be popular. Her soul was not free to advance in holiness until she let go of these worldly distractions.

  Consider: How do concerns about my appearance or my popularity distract me from my desire to become holy?

- Spiritual purification was an ongoing process for Saint Teresa. Up to a certain point in her life, she was passive about her spiritual journey, so she didn't progress. But after her conversion she actively worked to rid herself of obstacles to the love of God. This work paid off with an eternal reward.

  Consider: What bad habits, vices, and sins are obstacles to my love for God?

- Loving God was more than religious rhetoric for Saint Teresa. She backed her words with her actions. When she wrote about the importance of the virtues of humility and detachment, she knew from her own experience that developing these virtues helped her love God with her whole soul.

  Consider: How can I consciously try to cultivate humility and detachment?

- Teresa of Avila is one of the great spiritual masters on the subject of prayer. Through trial and error over the course of her life, she arrived at insights that she shares with us in her writings. Thanks to her efforts, we don't have to start from scratch to learn how to pray.

Consider: How could my prayer be more of a loving conversation with Jesus?

- Reforming the Carmelite order was no small task. Saint Teresa encountered resistance from Church authorities and her superiors. She dealt with slanderous attacks from her own sisters. The Discalced Carmelite order owes its identity in large part to Saint Teresa's perseverance in spite of such trials. She courageously forged ahead, trusting in the guidance of the Holy Spirit and relying on the grace of God.

  Consider: What obstacles have kept me from following the promptings of the Holy Spirit in my life?

chapter three

✴ SAINT TERESA BENEDICTA OF THE CROSS ✴
Loving God With Your Whole Mind

For the foolishness of God is wiser than men.
1 Corinthians 1:25

HER LIFE

Edith Stein's life story began on October 12, 1891, in Breslau, Germany (now Wroclow, Poland). Her parents were both devout Jews, though it was her mother, Auguste, who was responsible for Edith's religious formation, as Edith's father died when she was less than two years old. Left to care for her seven children and run the family lumber business, Auguste was very busy, but she managed to instill a strong sense of Jewish custom and belief in the Stein household. With this diligent mother as the role model of her youth, Edith grew up to be a hardworking and independent woman.

In the Stein family Edith played a special role, and not just because she was the youngest. She revealed early on, to the joy of her family, that she was an unusually bright girl. Her older brothers and sisters used to enjoy quizzing her in the parlor, asking questions that gave her a chance to show off her knowledge. She loved to win these little games of wit and intellect, because she yearned to prove she was the best and the smartest.

When occasionally she didn't emerge victorious, she would cry tears of rage. Even as a young girl she earned the affectionate if slightly patronizing title of "Edith, the *smart* one."[1]

Edith so enjoyed learning that at six years of age she begged to enter school, refusing kindergarten as being beneath her. Thus began a virtual love affair with studies and education. Edith almost felt more at home in school than in her own house. When she sat at a desk, it was as if the rest of the world ceased to exist. She was most herself when she was engaged in intellectual pursuits.

Edith especially enjoyed the thrill of figuring out difficult problems. Her penetrating, creative mind would persevere through a math problem until the truth came to light, and then she would whistle a little song of victory. Such energetic resilience in her studies helped develop the endurance that marked her tireless quest for truth as an adult.

Edith spent a large portion of her adolescence working toward academic success. Then, much to the surprise of those who knew her, she left school at the age of fifteen to move in with her older sister Else and help care for her children, giving her formal education an eight-month hiatus. Living with her sister's family was an education of a different sort. It gave Edith a new appreciation for domestic duties, the concrete operations of family life, and human life in general.

Edith took such lessons to heart but soon realized she wanted to return to her academic pursuits. Her educational journey would culminate in a PH.D. in philosophy *summa cum laude* at the age of twenty-six.

But the time away from her studies had a significant impact on Edith's life. During her stay with her sister and brother-in-law, she made a conscious decision to stop praying. She turned from the religion of her childhood and entered into a period of atheism. From the time she was fifteen until she turned twenty-one, Edith didn't believe in the existence of a personal God.

In spite of this lack of belief, however, Edith stayed consciously devoted to the pursuit of truth. This mission now replaced the unquestioning acceptance of her family's religious heritage. She had a deep longing to understand, in an intellectually satisfying way, the truth about reality and human existence. Many years would pass before she would discover that the truth she was looking for was not in her books but in the person of Jesus Christ.

The College Years

Edith's personal quest led her to study psychology when she first entered college. The "science of the mind" intrigued her. Through this discipline she hoped to rationally and scientifically arrive at a clear understanding of the soul as the center of the human person (an interesting goal for an atheist). But her professors at the University of Breslau disillusioned her: They were teaching that the soul did not exist.

Edith's sharp intellect did not passively accept whatever she was told, however. While other students might carelessly conform to the ideas of their professors, Edith always thought everything through for herself. Although she was eager to learn, she never allowed that eagerness to impede her ability to think critically. She believed careful, logical, analytical thinking would lead her to the truth. Little did she know at the time that her journey toward the truth of faith would start with a paradox, the paradox of the cross.

Much to her relief, Edith soon encountered the writings of a German philosopher named Edmund Husserl. Husserl's thought, which resonated clearly with Edith's critical mind, openly considered the workings of the human soul. Husserl was instrumental in a branch of philosophy called "phenomenology," which takes into rational consideration the "evidence" we gain through both natural and supernatural experience. This greatly appealed to Edith in her search for truth. So she left Breslau to study under Dr. Husserl at the University of Göttingen.

During her time at Göttingen, Edith entered into a thriving community of young intellectuals who would become some of her dearest friends. Many of these classmates were Christian or eventually converted to Christianity. The open-minded approach of phenomenology and the influence of these philosopher friends brought Edith to a new threshold on her personal journey. While she was not yet seeing with the eyes of faith, she was beginning to accept the *idea* that faith could be a source of knowledge. Her belief that all things had to be rationally and scientifically proven collapsed. "And there, standing in front of me, was the world of faith,"[2] she later wrote.

Edith was still a long way from the complete joy of her conversion, however. During the first year of her stay at Göttingen, she experienced a severe depression. She had read a book about university alcoholism and immorality that disturbed her so deeply that she seemed powerless to restore her former optimism about human existence. She felt extreme loneliness and despair, and she even had suicidal thoughts during this dark time of her life.

Edith persevered through this trial. After months of painful struggle, she had an experience that began to restore hope and help her break free of the darkness that had oppressed her. She describes the powerful moment that conquered her depression:

> I went about as one unbearably burdened, and I was beyond finding enjoyment in anything at all. What cured me of this depression is highly significant. That year a great Bach Festival was given.... I only know that Luther's defiant hymn "A Mighty Fortress" was included....
>
>> When in stirring battle cry, the verse was sung
>>> And though this world with devils filled
>>>> Should threaten to undo us,
>>>> We will not fear,
>>>> ...for truth will triumph through us.
>> My pessimistic outlook vanished completely.[3]

A reference to the power of truth brought light to Edith's darkened mind in the midst of this personal battle. Truth motivated her. Her immersion in academic pursuits, and even the period of her questioning atheism, sprang from her deep devotion to the truth. This constant, unwavering allegiance to truth would eventually lead Edith to Christianity, the Catholic Church, and the Carmelite order. As she wrote in her autobiography, "My desire for the truth was one sole prayer."[4]

Even when she thought she had given up praying, deep down Edith was still crying out to know the ultimate Truth. She would come to believe that anyone who is searching for truth is actually searching for God, whether they acknowledge it or not.

A Cause for Conversion

After breaking free from her depression, Edith entered into life with renewed vigor and enthusiasm. She was devoted to her studies and her classmates. She made trips back to Breslau to visit her family, paying special attention to her little nieces and nephews, who were very fond of their Aunt Edith. She loved to go hiking, dancing, and picnicking during these years. Once, when she was in charge of the menu for the picnic, she packed a lunch that consisted of nothing but chocolate pudding. Clearly the joy of life had returned!

Edith would soon leave all of this frivolity behind, however. World War I was raging, and in 1915, after passing her university examinations, she spent six months as a Red Cross nurse in a hospital for members of the Austrian army. When she returned from this service bearing a medal of valor, she began her work as Husserl's assistant. She developed a deep academic bond with her mentor, completing her doctoral thesis at the University of Fribourg, where Husserl now worked.

The sobering experience of working as an army nurse had its effect on Edith, but even more significant than those months of service were the losses she personally felt. Several of her beloved classmates were killed on the front. Among them was a young man named Adolf Reinach, whose *Notes on the Philosophy of Religion* contributed to Edith's acceptance of religious knowledge.

Adolf's widow, Anna, was also a dear friend of Edith. Shortly after her husband's death, Anna asked Edith to come to the Reinach home to help organize Adolf's writings and papers. Edith prepared herself for the visit, trying to muster up the courage and calm that she knew poor Anna would desperately need. Edith, however, was in for a surprise.

On arriving at the Reinach home, Edith found not a withered widow in the depths of misery but a woman of extraordinary peace and confidence. Even in the midst of her grief, it was Anna who comforted the sorrowing Edith! Anna explained her calm as the natural effect of her Christian faith, a faith that celebrates the triumph of life over death through the cross. Anna truly believed her husband was now enjoying eternal happiness with Jesus in heaven.

Edith had no intellectual categories to describe Anna's peace in the midst of such tremendous suffering. Scientific formulas and philosophical systems were not helpful in this moment of trial, but the lived experience of Christian faith brought great consolation. Edith now had a glimpse into something she had never seen before. Through the witness of Anna's belief in Jesus, the eyes of faith began to open for Edith. "It was my first encounter with the cross and the divine strength it gives those who bear it…. It was the moment in which my atheism collapsed…and Christ shone brightly: Christ in the mystery of the cross."[5]

Edith had been yearning to discover, understand, and articulate the truth. She had read, discussed, and studied tirelessly. But these pursuits, as noble as they were, could only bring her to the threshold of this new enlightenment that came through the cross. The cross lifted Anna (and Edith) beyond natural understanding to divine wisdom. Edith saw that the greatest truth is not an idea or a philosophy but a person, Jesus Christ.

For those who see only with the naked eye, the cross can be ugly and fearsome, but to the faithful Christian it is a sign of beauty and hope. Faith in the cross now began to allow Edith to go beyond natural understanding to supernatural understanding. Indeed, the cross would become the cornerstone of her life.

Growing Faith

Although Anna Reinach's witness had planted the seed, Edith's faith journey had only begun. She needed time to absorb this new insight, to consider all the options that lay before her. She wanted to be rooted in the truth, but she was not yet sure where to find its fullness. She wondered, for example, whether she should join the Lutheran Church of the Reinachs and many other friends or whether the Catholic Church was the one Christ had truly established.

She turned to the New Testament and began to read it for the first time in the light of faith. Within those pages Edith found a world full of realities that she had never considered in her scholarship and philosophical research. Over the next several years, she continued to learn about the Christian faith. She paid special attention to life experiences that provided insights relevant to her search. Three experiences in particular made a deep impression on Edith.

The first was a Catholic funeral service she attended, to pay her last respects to a well-known scientist. The overwhelming sense of peace and consolation pervading the service made a deep impression on Edith. This stood in contrast to previous experiences at non-Christian funeral services, which had left her with no anticipation of a joyful reunion after death. The Catholic service was full of hope. Combining this insight with her memory of Anna Reinach's amazing peace in the wake of her husband's death convinced Edith all the more of the Christian belief in the cross and the Resurrection.

On another occasion Edith was walking through the city of Frankfurt, and she noticed a woman stepping into the cathedral. Through the open doors Edith saw the woman kneel before the tabernacle in silent prayer, as if talking to a friend. Edith had never thought of going to the synagogue for anything other than formal religious services. But here was a woman who took a small pause in the midst of her daily activities, entering the Lord's house to have a personal conversation with him. Edith was beginning to realize that the truths of the Christian faith were deeply personal and full of hope and love.

Later Edith paid a summer visit to her friends Theodore and Hedwig Conrad-Martius. When her hosts went out for the evening, they left Edith with an invitation to make herself comfortable and to borrow anything from their extensive library. At random Edith selected a copy of Saint Teresa of Avila's autobiography. She was so taken with the book that she didn't put it down until she had finished it in the wee hours of the morning. With this reading Edith's long journey toward embracing the Christian faith came to a climax. As she recalled, "When I closed the book I said to myself: 'That is the truth!' "[6]

During his homily at Edith Stein's beatification in 1987, Pope John Paul II referred to this moment: "In that night she found truth—not the truth of philosophy, but rather the truth in person, the loving person of God. Edith Stein had sought the truth and found God."[7]

Edith's experience confirmed the original insight she had gained after her visit to Anna Reinach. The fullness of truth wasn't found in abstract thought or formulas but in the love that Jesus so perfectly revealed on the cross. Although human wisdom may struggle to comprehend this, the faithful acceptance of God's wisdom makes it possible to rejoice in the love of the crucified Christ. This is the truth that is meant to guide our lives. Saint Teresa of Avila knew this and responded to love with love; Edith Stein now intended to do the same.

Christian, Catechumen, Catholic

When making decisions, Edith was slow and careful. Her analytical mind weighed the pros and cons before she acted on any idea. But once she decided on a course of action, she didn't hesitate to embrace it and follow through, even if the idea met with resistance.

This had been the case with her move to Göttingen, which meant leaving her family for the first time, much to their chagrin. She also revealed this perseverance in her decision to serve as an army nurse, a choice her mother had vehemently discouraged. Now three years had passed since Edith's experience at the Reinachs'. With her reading of Saint Teresa of Avila, it was time to act.

The day after reading *The Life of Saint Teresa of Avila*, Edith went out and bought a Catholic catechism and a missal. She devoted herself to studying Catholicism and soon went to Mass for the first time. After Mass ended Edith approached the priest and asked him for baptism. He informed Edith that she needed to be instructed in the faith first, to which she replied, "Test my knowledge."[8]

And he did. The pastor was impressed with Edith's comprehension of Church doctrine. He arranged for her to be baptized on the first day of the coming year, after she received formal instruction. On January 1, 1922, Edith Stein was received into the Catholic Church.

Edith did not see her choice to follow Christ as a rejection of the religion of her childhood. On the contrary, she believed Jesus was the Messiah whom her Jewish upbringing had taught her to expect. Like the twelve apostles, she saw Christianity as the fulfillment of the Jewish faith.

Edith's family, however, struggled with her decision. Her conversion was especially disheartening for her mother. Edith would not abandon her newfound faith, but she was sensitive to her family's resistance. After reading more of Saint Teresa of Avila's works, she felt that God was calling her to enter the Carmelite order, but out of respect for her mother, she would wait twelve years before entering the convent.

This was also the advice of a trusted priest, who believed Edith had much to give to the Church as a layperson. And indeed she made many valuable contributions as she proceeded to direct her life toward growth in holiness and service to the Church.

Keeping the Faith

Embracing Catholicism was more than an internal experience for Edith. Her life's goals now took on a different dimension. She had once dreamt of being a philosophy professor, but now she decided to leave behind the pursuit of a scholarly career (she had already encountered many roadblocks because she was a woman) and happily accepted a position as a German teacher at a Dominican school for young women in Speyer. Freed from unquestioning allegiance to the scientific worldview, Edith now began to apply her mind to prayer and a deepening understanding of eternal truth.

At Speyer Edith lived a structured life of activity and contemplation, modeled in large part on the life of the Dominican sisters with whom she lived. Although she hadn't taken any public vows, she kept personal vows of poverty, chastity, and obedience. She lived simply, taking little pay for her work other than what she needed for food, lodging, and clothing. She prayed the Liturgy of the Hours regularly and loved to participate in the liturgical life of the Church.

During this time at Speyer, Edith began to read the writings of Saint Thomas Aquinas. She worked on a translation of Aquinas's *Quaestiones Disputatae De Veritate*, "Disputed Questions on Truth." Clearly she and Saint Thomas shared a common interest! The renowned philosopher and theologian opened Edith's eyes to the harmonious interplay of faith and reason. Having accepted Christianity and incorporated her faith into her philosophical worldview, Edith Stein elaborated upon these themes in several works, including a dialogue she composed between Aquinas and Edmund Husserl, comparing and contrasting their philosophical approaches.

With her newfound openness to intertwining faith and reason, Edith moved on to the next phase of her life. After eight years at Speyer, she accepted a position as a teacher at the German Institute of Scientific Pedagogy in Münster. Her life now became a whirlwind of lectures, both at the institute and beyond. She frequently traveled and spoke on, among other things, the role of women in culture and in the Church, offering a refreshing vision that integrated Catholicism and healthy feminism.

Had Edith gone against her spiritual advisor's directive and entered the convent immediately after her conversion, she may not have had the opportunity to present these inspiring and insightful lectures. But Edith wasn't meant to be a laywoman in the world forever. God was calling her to himself through a Carmelite vocation, and the time had come for Edith to respond to that call.

From Novice to Nun

After a year in her position at Münster, Edith had to leave the institute. Adolf Hitler had come to power in January of 1933, and by April the Nazis had forbidden Edith to teach because of her Jewish heritage. Her conversion to Christianity could not protect her from the devastating injustices Hitler's Reich was inflicting on the Jewish people.

Although this was difficult, Edith rejoiced, because she believed God was closing doors for her effectiveness in the outside world so she could enter the seclusion of Carmel without concern. The only obstacle remaining was the difficulty of informing her mother.

The blow was a harsh one for Auguste Stein. She felt that by converting to Christianity her daughter had already abandoned her family and the Jewish people at the worst possible moment. Wasn't it enough that Edith had chosen baptism into the Catholic Church? Why did she have to go so far as to enter the convent?

Edith tried to explain that her entrance into Carmel didn't mean rejecting her family or her heritage, but her mother could not bear it. Edith's decision was so difficult for Auguste that neither she nor any of Edith's siblings attended the momentous celebration when Edith received her Carmelite habit. For months Auguste refused to reply to any of Edith's weekly letters. The pain Edith caused her family in following God's call was a challenging cross for her to bear.

As she entered the Carmelite novitiate under these tumultuous circumstances, Edith knew that trial and suffering were going to be part of her future. Even convent life presented trials. She had to keep to the strict schedule. She had to learn to do household chores and domestic duties that did not come naturally to her. (A bit clumsy, she had difficulty managing a broom at first.) Dr. Stein, the well-known and sought-after lecturer and teacher, also had to humble herself to sit in beginners' classes with other novices only half her age. But she joyfully embraced her new situation.

Edith had come to understand that because of the cross, she could offer up her suffering and pain as a prayer. She had an especially strong sense that God was inviting her to offer sacrifices on behalf of the Jewish people, to unite their terrible sufferings to the cross of Jesus. Edith chose the religious name Sister Teresa Benedicta of the Cross because of her devotion to the power of the cross and her love for the Benedictine order (a love that had grown through her connections with a Benedictine monastery).

Edith would live as Sister Teresa Benedicta for close to nine years. Those years were difficult because of the horrors taking place under the Nazi regime. Even the walls of Carmel could not protect her from the tragedies surrounding her.

Edith and her sister Rosa, who had converted to Catholicism and become a secular Carmelite after their mother's death, moved to a Carmelite convent in Holland in 1942 to avoid the Nazi threat in Germany. However, when the Dutch bishops issued a public statement against the Nazis, the sisters' safety was threatened again. This time their Catholic identity was part of the risk, as the Nazis were taking retribution on Catholics of Jewish descent. As the S.S. arrived to take Edith and Rosa to Amersfoort Prison Camp, Edith said to her sister, "Come, let us go for our people."[9]

The Nazis deported Edith and Rosa to Auschwitz on August 1, 1942. On August 9 Edith Stein was martyred in the gas chamber.

The soldiers who carried out their orders to eliminate this woman probably thought she was gone forever. Little did they know that her legacy would live on long after her body had breathed its last. Through her writings, which have steadily grown in popularity since her death, Edith continues to teach a wide spectrum of students, including us.

Unlike Thérèse of Lisieux and Teresa of Avila, Edith didn't tend to share publicly the private workings of God in her soul. She wrote no extensive spiritual memoirs, and she referred to her conversion simply as "my secret for me alone."[10] Consistent with her philosophical inclinations, she usually spoke in abstract, objective terms, not in personal, subjective ones. So what we learn of her we learn from the events of her life that we have just examined, taken together with her philosophical and devotional writings.

Edith Stein's lived example has given us insight into loving Jesus with our whole mind. Through her lifelong journey she came to trust in his wisdom instead of her own. In addition to living this love, in her writings Edith addressed the idea of surrendering our mind to divine wisdom. She wrote specifically on three important themes: 1) the unity of faith and reason, 2) the wisdom of God, and 3) suffering and the cross.

The Unity of Faith and Reason

The writings of Saint Thomas Aquinas helped Edith discover the value of philosophy as a tool for discovering the mysteries of God within creation. With the guidance of the Angelic Doctor, Edith unified her identity as a philosopher with her identity as a believer. She realized she didn't need to reject intellectual or philosophical knowledge; instead she could put this knowledge at the service of truth.

Her work from this time on was such that Pope John Paul II, in his encyclical *Fides et Ratio*, praised her for helping enrich the process of philosophical enquiry by taking faith into consideration. Her dialogue between Husserl and Aquinas, along with her *Finite and Eternal Being*, helped earn Edith this distinction. Within their pages Edith elaborates on the connection between philosophical knowledge and the truths of faith.

In the dialogue between Aquinas and Husserl, Edith's ideas emerge through the mouthpiece of Aquinas, who dominates the conversation. According to Saint Thomas (and now Edith), faith is a way to access truths that would otherwise be closed to us. Faith gives us *more* information; it doesn't eliminate any we already have.

Edith believed that faith enriches our knowledge because it offers us something new, over and above our natural experience. She realized that there are elements of truth that philosophy cannot grasp apart from the light of faith. Science and philosophy are valuable—they give us partial access to truth—but they stop short of the fullness of supernatural truth. Accepting what supersedes our natural understanding brings a deeper enlightenment. According to Edith, if philosophy honestly seeks the truth, it can't ignore the knowledge we access through faith, because all truth is interrelated.

Edith further discusses this idea in her major work, *Finite and Eternal Being*. Here Edith argues that the noblest task of a Christian philosopher is to prepare the way for supernatural truth. She believed that the perfect fulfillment of philosophy, which aims at wisdom, is the divine wisdom itself.

In this same work Edith explains that God may raise human beings above their natural ways of thinking to a totally different level of knowledge. This elevation, she believed, enables them to share in the divine vision that beholds all things in one simple glance. Faith expands the horizons of our knowledge, allowing us to be literally open-minded.

Edith knew that many people can be closed-minded regarding matters of faith. Embracing the limited worldview that once held her captive, they accept only the truths of science and philosophy. This mentality leads some people to reject faith. Edith called this deliberate rejection of faith "a state of blindness."[11] She believed in the value of expanding her mind to include not only scientific analysis but *all* of reality.

The Wisdom of God

Edith Stein teaches us that the philosophical pursuit of truth finds its completion in the wisdom of God and that loving God with the whole mind is not merely an intellectual process. Some may assume that for an intellectual such as herself, conversion came through discovering the seamless logical arguments in defense of the Christian faith, of which there are plenty. But as we have seen, it was the mysterious power of the cross, not an intellectual theory, that brought this philosopher to her knees. She had to move beyond her human understanding and humbly submit her mind to the wisdom of God. As Saint Paul said when he preached about the cross, even the *foolishness* of God is wiser than human wisdom (see 1 Corinthians 1:25). So certainly the *wisdom* of God far exceeds our simple grasp.

In the deeper forms of prayer, with which much of Carmelite spirituality is concerned, we open our minds to God's wisdom. Through prayer Edith came into living contact with God. She experienced him in a more profound way than just hearing about him or learning about the things he has done. Coming to know God personally allowed her mind to embrace a new kind of knowledge.

In her essay "Ways to Know God," Edith compares natural knowledge of God to knowing about a person's existence because of things like photographs, writings, and other people's stories. But knowing God through supernatural experience (which comes through prayer) is like actually meeting a person. Personal knowledge allows the mind to grasp the deeper reality of who the person is, not reducing him or her to a collection of facts and reports. Faith, with the supernatural knowledge it gives us, is the bridge between natural knowledge of God and supernatural *experience* of him.

As a Carmelite nun Edith was well practiced in meeting God personally through contemplative prayer. In this form of prayer, the mind's normal activity is put at the service of loving God, who lifts the mind up to a supernatural plane.

Contemplation offers insights that far surpass anything we could arrive at by our own power. In such prayer the mind can have a small share in the glory of divine knowledge. This knowledge is "unending, infinite fullness at rest,"[12] as Edith put it. She believed that contemplation elevates the mind to share in heavenly knowledge. Hence divine illumination can make a plain, uneducated person wiser than the most educated scholar. As Edith wrote, "It depends on [God]… to raise man above his natural mode of thinking to a quite different manner of knowing."[13]

This "different manner of knowing" was a focus of Edith's great work *The Science of the Cross*. Edith was fascinated with Saint John of the Cross, whose writings were the inspiration for the work. He makes frequent reference to the "dark" knowledge of faith, because as our natural modes of thinking surrender to God's wisdom, we experience a kind of darkness. This surrender can be frightening, because we do not yet know by experience what lies on the other side of our surrender.

The knowledge that supersedes human understanding comes through a certain "darkening" of our natural thought processes. Accepting supernatural knowledge requires us to progress beyond the comfort of predictable axioms and formulas. But in return we receive a new light, the light of faith, a light that dawns when the dark night has passed.

Edith quotes Saint John of the Cross: "For through the intellect you receive wisdom concerning one, two or three truths; however, in the light of faith, the soul receives, at once, all of God's wisdom, that is, the Son of God, who communicates himself to her in faith."[14]

Jesus is the fullness of divine wisdom. Accepting him, submitting our whole heart, soul, and mind to him, allows the wisdom of God to guide us. Edith was quick to note, however, that accepting this wisdom also means accepting the cross.

Suffering and the Cross

The "folly" of the cross, as Saint Paul called it (see 1 Corinthians 1:21–25), was essential to Edith Stein's conversion. Our ways are not God's ways, and our wisdom falls infinitely short of his (see Isaiah 55:8–9). The cross is the supreme sign of this. What appears to us to be the end may be only the beginning of God's almighty plan.

The power of the cross overcame what seemed insurmountable: death. Through this unexpected power Edith Stein first came to accept Jesus. And united to the suffering of the cross, she finally offered her life to him in martyrdom.

Following her experience with Anna Reinach, Edith learned that the cross had the power to transform suffering into joy. She believed that helping Christ carry his cross fills us with peace and strength. Earthly logic cannot explain this truth; rather God reveals this to those who humbly accept his wisdom.

Because of the significance of the cross in Edith's understanding of the faith, she wrote about it in a number of her religious essays, including "Love of the Cross" and "Exaltation of the Cross." She did not fear suffering in union with Jesus, nor did she shy away from it. She understood that embracing it was a fundamental element of the Christian call. She urges us to remember this: "[T]he Savior today looks at us, solemnly probing us, and asks each one of us: Will you remain faithful to the Crucified?"[15]

Indeed, Christ instructed all those who follow him about the centrality of the cross. As Edith wrote, "[W]e are to recall the challenge of the Lord: Anyone who would follow me must take up his cross."[16]

Having experienced suffering of many varieties in her life—the loss of her father as a young girl, the depression of her youth, the tragedy of war, the disapproval of her family, the discrimination of the Nazis—Edith was not naïve. The radically unique Christian understanding of suffering inspired her. Instead of trying to explain suffering, ignore it, escape it, or rage against it, she found in the Christian faith a significance to suffering: It is a share in the redemptive power of Christ.

In light of this vision, what may have appeared meaningless to Edith now had meaning; what might have seemed a waste now had infinite value. Faith offered her the choice to go beyond natural appearances to accept a deeper wisdom about suffering.

She came to understand that one might even *choose* to suffer, offering up some particular sacrifice as a prayer. As Edith wrote, such an action "is not merely a pious reminder of the suffering of the Lord. Voluntary expiatory suffering is what truly and really unites one to the Lord intimately."[17]

Submitting her mind to the deeper truths of the faith was not enough for Edith. She also wanted to submit her actions to the wisdom of God. Offering up sacrifices was a concrete way to demonstrate that she believed in something greater than human wisdom.

But for all this suffering, Edith was not a gloomy saint. Rather she took joy in the cross. She wrote:

> [B]ecause *being* one with Christ is our sanctity, and progressively *becoming* one with him our happiness on earth, the love of the cross in no way contradicts being a joyful child of God.... To suffer and to be happy although suffering, to have one's feet on the earth, to walk on the dirty and rough paths of this earth and yet to be enthroned with Christ at the Father's right hand, to laugh and cry with the children of this world and ceaselessly sing the praises of God with the choirs of angels—this is the life of the Christian until the morning of eternity breaks forth.[18]

These words capture the surprising nature of a faith that unapologetically embraces the paradox of the cross. This same faith proclaims confidently that God became a human, that a virgin gave birth, that bread and wine become the Body and Blood of Christ, that Jesus rose from the dead, and that eternal life is real. Edith Stein teaches us that fully living out our faith means joyfully submitting our mind to these supernatural mysteries.

LIVING THE LESSONS

Edith Stein understood that truth and love are deeply inter-twined. Her love for God was born out of her search for the truth. Once her mind embraced her Savior, she was able to love him so fervently that she wanted nothing more than to be close to him. She wrote:

> One thing alone is certain: that God is
> And that his hand holds us in being.
> Then even if around us the whole world falls to wrack and ruin,
> We are not ruined if we hold ourselves to him.[19]

Edith had come to realize that uniting ourselves to God, even in those times when we don't comprehend everything going on around us, is a certain path to peace and security. All the great questions and trials of life lose their ability to disturb us when we rest in the knowledge that God himself walks with us. This understanding of reality, this faithful surrender of our lives, helps us to calmly accept the unknown.

Not only do we live with the mysteries of our own lives, but the most important elements of the faith are also mysteries—the Trinity, the Incarnation, the Resurrection, the sacraments, and so on. These spiritual realities are so deep that we cannot wrap our minds completely around them. God knows this. He revealed these things to us; he didn't expect us to figure them out on our own. He gave us Jesus to show us eternal truth—God's wisdom.

Surrendering our minds to Jesus can be difficult and hum-bling, as it was for Edith Stein. She needed humility to surrender her brilliant mind to the wisdom of God. Yet she never regretted choosing the obedience of faith, and neither will we. Edith knew that Jesus was the Light of the World and the enlightenment of her mind. This knowledge can transform us as well. When we open our minds to the light of faith, we can enter into new realms of knowledge and understanding, as God takes our thoughts, our intellect, our memory, and our imagination exactly where he wants them to go.

This will never mean denying scientific or philosophical truth; truth cannot contradict itself. But it will allow new horizons to spread out before us. We will see farther—and clearer—than we could ever see on our own. The saints' minds were open to this supernatural expanse. These holy models were "easily and joyfully led and molded,"[20] as Edith describes, by the power of God. They didn't keep a selfish and possessive hold on the powers of their minds but offered their entire beings to God because of their great love for him.

Through her life of prayer and meditation, Saint Teresa Benedicta of the Cross came closer and closer to the wisdom of God. The insights of faith offered her mind an abundance of new material for consideration and reflection. She describes the fruit of this meditation as "tranquil, peaceful, loving surrender in the presence of God whom [the soul] has come to know through faith."[21]

Saint Teresa Benedicta's grace-filled journey brought her to value the love of God above all philosophical investigation and debate. Her life's quest led her, through faith, to "the simple embrace of the one Truth."[22] She realized that giving our minds to God is more than an intellectual surrender: It is an opportunity to rest forever in the fullness of Truth and Love.

For Reflection

- Which qualities of Saint Teresa Benedicta of the Cross do I most admire?
- How could these qualities become part of who I am?

Ten Ways to Be More Like Saint Teresa Benedicta of the Cross

1. Pray the Liturgy of the Hours.
2. Make an annual silent retreat.
3. Study the history and customs of the Jewish people.
4. Attend lectures on religious topics.
5. Make the Sign of the Cross when you pass a Catholic church.
6. Make Scripture and other spiritual reading a part of your daily life.
7. Help an overwhelmed mother so she can be refreshed in her vocation.
8. Celebrate the Feast of the Triumph of the Cross, September 14.
9. Study the *Catechism of the Catholic Church* and the writings of Teresa of Avila, John of the Cross, and Thomas Aquinas.
10. Say a prayer of thanks to God for the grace of baptism.

Points for Consideration

- If Edith Stein had catered to other people's opinions, she wouldn't have become Saint Teresa Benedicta of the Cross. Her decision to convert brought opposition, criticism, and even rejection from friends and family. A strictly rational perspective wouldn't have endured these social pressures for the sake of an invisible God. But Edith trusted that the wisdom of God was greater than human wisdom, and thus a saint was born.

Consider: How much do I struggle when I face social opposition to my decisions?

- The cross was a solution, not a problem, for Saint Teresa Benedicta. It offered a solution to the problem of suffering; it transformed what might have been meaningless into something redemptive. Saint Teresa Benedicta did not become bitter about the sorrows or even the tragedies of her life, because she relied on the power of the cross.

  Consider: How do I respond to Christ's call to take up the cross in my life?

- As a convert to Christianity, Saint Teresa Benedicta never lost appreciation for her faith: She didn't take it for granted, and she never considered it to be mundane or dull. Having made the decision to follow Christ consciously and deliberately, she clung to the faith with energy and enthusiasm. She understood what a precious gift it was to know, love, and serve Jesus Christ.

  Consider: How do I show my gratitude for the gift of being a Christian?

- Saint Teresa Benedicta took genuine consolation in the thought of heaven. For her it was a source of hope and comfort in the midst of life's trials and surely at the moment before her death. For Saint Teresa Benedicta and all the martyrs, belief in heaven helped them have the strength and courage to act heroically.

Consider: How much does belief in heaven console me during times of trial?

- Saint Teresa Benedicta understood the gift of the Bible in a special way. Because of her Jewish upbringing, she had a deep appreciation for the way in which the New Testament fulfills the Old Testament. Once she had put her faith in Christ, she also accepted the truth of his Word and oriented her life accordingly.

  Consider: How does God's revelation through Sacred Scripture shape my actions and choices?

chapter four

※ BLESSED TERESA OF CALCUTTA ※
Loving Your Neighbor as Yourself

*"Lord, when did we see you hungry and feed you, or
thirsty and give you drink?"*
…*"I say to you, as you did it to one of the least of these
my brethren, you did it to me."*
Matthew 25:37, 40

HER LIFE

Gonxha (Agnes) Bojaxhiu was born on August 26, 1910, in
Skopje, a city in former Yugoslavia, to Albanian parents. She was
the fifth child of Nicholas and Rosa, but only she, her sister Aga,
and her brother Lazar survived beyond infancy.

Nurtured by the love between Nicholas and Rosa, the young
Bojaxhiu family flourished. During the day their devoted mother
cared for the children while their father was at work. When evening approached, Rosa would rush about and prepare to greet
Nicholas. No matter what had happened during the day, Rosa
was always smiling when Nicholas returned home. Growing
up in the midst of this joyful existence was a pleasure for Aga,
Lazar, and Agnes.

These days of bliss were numbered, however. Nicholas was a
prominent businessman involved in local politics. His political
activity may have been connected to his sudden death, which

many suspected was due to poisoning. Agnes was only seven years old. Rosa was now entirely responsible for her children, and while the home had always been a devout one, it now began to radiate even more clearly the light of the faith.

The Bojaxhius were active in the parish church across the street from their home, Sacred Heart of Jesus. The widow and her children regularly participated in church meetings, religious services, and the choir. Agnes was a gifted soprano and the soloist for the choir. She was also an active member of the Daughters of Mary, and she faithfully attended her catechism classes. She relished every opportunity to learn about her favorite topics: the lives of the saints and the work of missionaries.

The faith of the family extended beyond the walls of the church. When poor beggars came to the door of the Bojaxhiu home, Rosa never allowed them to go away hungry. She explained to her three children that these people, poor though they were, were their brothers and sisters too. This Christian perspective made an impact on the youngsters, who grew up serving the poor. Agnes would eventually make this her life's work.

Agnes had a special interest in missionary service. As a young girl she eagerly absorbed any news of missionary activity. Whenever she heard of a new missionary endeavor, she would locate the mission site on a map of the world that hung in her house and record little notes next to it. She followed the reports of Christian men and women working in far-off places, hoping one day to join their company.

When she was twelve years old, Agnes told her mother she wanted to be a missionary, but Rosa said she needed to wait until she was older. Six years later Agnes was ready to assert that her long-standing desire was more than a child's fancy. While offering prayers at an altar in honor of Mary, the Patroness of Skopje, Agnes felt her vocation confirmed in her heart. She believed that Mary had interceded for her to help her know her vocation with certainty. Agnes's call to religious life and attraction to missionary service would soon lead her to her home in India.

At eighteen years of age, Agnes waved good-bye to her little family, whom she would never see again, and she stepped onto the train alone. Traveling through Yugoslavia, Austria, Switzerland, France, and England, she arrived safely at the motherhouse of the Sisters of Our Lady of Loreto in Dublin, Ireland. This was the missionary teaching order she had decided to join.

Agnes studied English for two months before boarding a ship for India, which arrived there thirty-seven days later. After spending one week in Calcutta, Agnes traveled to the novitiate house in Darjeeling, India. Two years more, and Agnes took her religious name, Mary Teresa (after Saint Thérèse of Lisieux, whom she referred to as "the Little Teresa," in contrast to Teresa of Avila, "the Big Teresa"[1]).

After making her temporary vows, Sister Teresa went to Calcutta for her first assignment. She moved to the pristine campus of St. Mary's High School, which served girls from wealthy Indian families. During her first years there, Sister Teresa taught history and geography. Later she served as the director of studies.

Sister Teresa was quite content at St. Mary's, where she would spend seventeen years. She embraced her new home and culture to such an extent that she would later declare herself to be "Indian by choice."[2] She considered herself the happiest nun in the community, though her life there was one of routine responsibility. She prayed and taught, and then she did it again the next day. The sisters who lived with her considered her to be ordinary, quiet, and shy.

But on September 10, 1946, something out of the ordinary took place in Sister Teresa's life. On this day, which she later referred to as "Inspiration Day,"[3] she heard God speak to her while she was traveling by train to Darjeeling. She understood that God was asking her to start a new order of missionary sisters who would work among the poorest of the poor in India. But she did not know how she was to carry out this divine directive. "I knew where I belonged," she later said, "but I did not know how to get there."[4]

This dramatic "call within a call" persisted. Sister Teresa felt that God was asking her, "Wouldst thou not help?"[5] This was not her own whim or idea: She firmly believed Jesus was making this request, and she wanted to respond with generous love.

In a letter to Archbishop Perier dated January of 1947, Sister Teresa explained how she had heard God asking her to begin an order of Indian sisters to serve the poor, and she asked for the archbishop's permission to do so. In spite of her desire to begin this work, however, she respectfully wrote, "[A]t one word that Your Grace would say, I am ready never to consider again any of those strange thoughts which have been coming continually."[6] Thankfully, Archbishop Perier did not tell her to abandon the idea. But it would be some time before she was able to carry out the call God had placed in her heart.

Sister Teresa had no intention of giving up her religious vows, but she did need permission to leave her religious community. She planned to start an entirely new order, which required additional ecclesiastical sanction. After several years marked by letters and visits to obtain special permission from the arch-bishop of Calcutta, the mother general of the Loreto nuns, and the Holy Father, Pope Pius XII, Sister Teresa was finally ready to say farewell to her convent home.

On August 17, 1948, Sister Teresa left behind the beautiful buildings and gardens of St. Mary's School, the community of sisters and students who had become her friends, and the comfort of stability and routine. She took off the religious habit she had worn for twenty years, donned the white sari of the poorest Indian women, and walked out into the streets of Calcutta.

Once again she was beginning an unknown journey alone. In fact, Mother Teresa later said that this was the most difficult thing she ever did in her life; it was more challenging even than leaving her family and her country to become a nun. And she did it for the love of God.

A New Mission

After taking a course in nursing, Sister Teresa conducted classes for children. Gathering them together in the open air, she taught the basics of personal hygiene and then gave lessons in the faith. At the beginning this makeshift school was truly humble: dirt and sticks had to suffice in place of paper and pencils. In spite of the scarcity of proper materials, however, the children came to love Sister Teresa, and the crowds grew each day.

Soon Sister Teresa was paying personal visits to the children's families. As she walked through the slums on these missions of charity, she witnessed extreme destitution. Those families who dwelt in ramshackle huts were the lucky ones; many people were living on the streets or in the gutters. Most of these forgotten men and women were on the verge of death, laying miserably without so much as a sympathetic glance from another human being to bring them comfort. But Sister Teresa did not ignore them. Her attentiveness to people in the direst situations became the hallmark of her work.

She recalled the moment when she first picked up a woman whom she saw in the street. "I could not have been a Missionary of Charity if I had passed by when I saw and smelt that woman who was eaten up by rats—her face, her legs. But I returned, picked her up and took her to a hospital."[7] It was not as simple as handing the woman over to the doctors, however; at first the hospital would not admit the woman. But Sister Teresa refused to move until they accepted the dying patient.

Next Sister Teresa approached the city authorities and asked for a place to bring the suffering people she was passing in the streets. They gave her an empty building in a Hindu temple, which she filled with patients within twenty-four hours.

And so the Society of the Missionaries of Charity was born. In the next months several young women came to join in Sister Teresa's work, all of them her former students from St. Mary's. They were eager to give themselves to God through this special mission. With their help Sister Teresa soon set up her first school. Then came a home for the sick and the dying, *Nirmal Hriday,* "Home of the Pure Heart." The building immediately filled to capacity with suffering people for whom the sisters lovingly cared. It didn't take long for Sister Teresa to become known as Mother Teresa, or simply Mother.

The sisters did not have a convent at first; they lived simply in a rented apartment. Within two years the Missionaries of Charity, with its twelve original members, had gained pontifical approval. Trusting entirely in God's providence to sustain their work, in only three years they had built a motherhouse, established an orphanage, and set up a program to serve lepers throughout the city of Calcutta. Twelve years later they opened their first home outside of India. By 1971 the order ran fifty homes throughout the world, and many more were yet to come. Mother Teresa once told several sisters who were about to begin a new mission, "If there are poor people on the moon, we will go there."[8]

She went on to help found the Missionary Brothers of Charity and two contemplative branches, the Missionary Brothers and Sisters of the Word. She also worked to establish the Coworkers, who support the Missionaries of Charity by offering prayers and resources for the work of the order.

With such productivity one might assume everything came easily to Mother Teresa. Not so. She dealt with opposition and resistance from political authorities as well as the ongoing challenge of caring for the poor and sick without any regular income for her order. On a personal level she also endured decades of intense spiritual darkness as well as physical pain and trauma.

When she was seventy-eight, she suffered from heart problems, likely aggravated by exhaustion from her work. Her doctors installed a pacemaker, and Pope John Paul II asked her to take concern for her health. She took six months of rest. Within another year she stepped down as superior general of the order, but five months later she was reinstalled.

Mother Teresa never fully recovered her health. She suffered five heart attacks before she finally rested in peace. She died on September 5, 1997, at the motherhouse in Calcutta, which had long since become her home. Several months before her death, she had appointed Sister Nirmala as the new head of the

Missionaries of Charity. Under Sister Nirmala's prayerful leadership, the order continues to flourish.

The Media Missionary

The loving work of the Missionaries of Charity, under the headship of Mother Teresa, has drawn much acclaim and attention through the years, although this was never a goal of the order. Mother Teresa met with royalty, world leaders, and the pope, not for personal glory but to discuss ways to help the poor and to urge these influential people to use their power for the sake of justice.

When she won prestigious awards—such as the Nobel Peace Prize, the Templeton Award for Progress in Religion, and the Pope John XXIII Peace Prize, for example—she would only accept them on behalf of the poor. Mother Teresa did not want to be the focal point on prize-giving day. She believed Christ was just using her as an instrument to unite the people who came to these awards ceremonies.

In accepting the Nobel Prize, Mother Teresa (who declined a banquet and used the money budgeted for one to feed the poor) expressed her view on the importance of loving our neighbors: "We cannot say, 'I love God, but I don't love my neighbor.'... How can you love God whom you do not see, if you don't love the neighbor whom you do see—the neighbor you know and live with every day?"[9]

Mother Teresa was a celebrity in spite of herself. It would be a challenge to find someone who doesn't know her name or recognize her face. Her image hangs in classrooms, churches, and homes. Books about her life line the shelves at bookstores and libraries. Documentaries about her work air on television. But Mother Teresa wasn't a fan of all the attention. She would occasionally tell interviewers that if she made it straight to heaven, it would be because of the journalists and photographers who made her go through purgatory before she died!

Although she disliked the publicity, it left a valuable legacy. Not only can we read multitudes of books on Mother Teresa's life and work and look up the texts of her many speeches and letters, but we also can hear her voice and see her face. This woman has inspired a change of heart in many people.

One man was contemplating suicide when he passed a shop with televisions that were playing scenes of Mother Teresa's work in the home for the dying. For the first time in many years, he felt that God still loved the world. He knelt down, prayed, and turned his life back to God. He later wrote Mother Teresa and told her about the effect this scene had on his life.

In addition to offering such inspiration, Mother Teresa's public accessibility helps bring us into a deeper understanding of her interior life. Much of the information we have about her comes through interviews she had during the course of her life as well as lectures she gave. We also gain insights from her letters, especially those she wrote to the Missionaries of Charity and to her spiritual director. The reports of people who worked with her or observed her consistently reveal her total devotion to the mission of loving her neighbors.

Mother Teresa saw and loved many "neighbors" in horrifying conditions. But instead of focusing on the wounds and the maggots crawling on a dying man's body, she would focus on his grateful smile after he received a plate of rice. Mother Teresa's love for Jesus enabled her to show joy and grace in the midst of repulsive circumstances.

This wrinkled woman who embraced such ugly situations was surprisingly attractive to the entire world. She captivated

Christians and non-Christians alike. We revere her for her tireless work and admire her for her generosity. She is a favorite reference point for causes of social concern.

Yet Mother Teresa was much more than a humanitarian in a white sari. Because of her continual focus on Jesus, her service was not simply social work. She specifically warned of the danger of doing the work for the sake of the work instead of for the love of Jesus. People were attracted to her not just because of a remarkable display of compassion; Mother Teresa was a magnet to humanity because she gave us a glimpse into the divine. She radiated the supernatural light of Christ that had begun to shine in her years before she entered the limelight.

This tiny woman with the courage of a giant sacrificed her family, her country, and her comfortable religious life to follow God's call. She gave up everything for the love of Jesus and served her neighbors as a response to that same love. She lived a life of continual service for over seven decades. Hers was a lifetime of selfless generosity, most of which she voluntarily spent in the midst of squalor and destitution for the sake of loving her neighbors as God called her to do.

Her Lessons

Mother Teresa loved God without reserve. She made a personal vow in 1942 never to refuse God anything. Because she lived this vow so generously, God's love extended to others through her. She knew that loving our neighbors as ourselves is intimately tied to loving God with our whole heart, soul, and mind. She believed this connection was so close that God made the commandment of loving our neighbors of the same importance as the first commandment.

As we seek to imitate Mother Teresa's tremendous love for

others by learning more about her teachings, three themes emerge: 1) the centrality of Christ, 2) the importance of the Eucharist, and 3) the presence of joy.

The Centrality of Christ

In her teachings about the central role of Christ in her life and work, there are several recurrent themes: the call to holiness, the power of prayer, quenching the thirst of Christ, and the distressing disguise of the poor.

The call to holiness. While Mother Teresa resisted any claims about her sanctity, those who recognized a heavenly light shining through her practically canonized her before she died. At times people asked her how she felt about this lofty reputation. To questions like these she often responded by teasing her interviewer—"Let me die first," she once said[10]—or by simply reaffirming that being holy is nothing extraordinary but rather just what God created us to be. "Holiness is not a luxury but a simple duty for you and me,"[11] she would say. Every human person has the innate capacity for holiness; that's how God designed us.

The Second Vatican Council specifically taught about the universal call to holiness. Mother Teresa knew well the constant teaching of the Church that the council clarified in declaring, "It is therefore quite clear that all Christians in any state or walk of life are called to the fullness of Christian life and to the perfection of love."[12] She liked to remind laypeople that God was calling them to belong entirely to him.

Some members of the laity have a tendency to think that priests and nuns have a special privilege for becoming truly holy or being declared saints. We are rightly disappointed when someone in a religious vocation does not live up to their calling. But if our tendency is to excuse our own sinful behavior sooner than we excuse that of a priest or nun, we are forgetting that God holds all of us to the same standard. When people sin— priests, nuns, husbands, wives, children, or anyone else—they fall short of their own call to holiness.

According to Mother Teresa, it takes nothing unusual to follow this calling other than Christ's help, which he offers freely to all of us. She always insisted that she did not have any special qualities, that the work she did was just Christ's work. "I am like a little pencil in His hand, that is all. He does the thinking. He does the writing."[13] She believed sanctity is nothing but Jesus intimately living in us.

Time and time again Mother Teresa revealed the secret to her success: "My secret is very simple: I pray."[14] All the work she did sprang from her relationship with Jesus, strengthened as it was every day in prayer.

The power of prayer. Mother Teresa did not mince words when it came to the value of prayer: "We need prayer just like we need air. Without prayer, we can do nothing."[15] She believed anyone can be holy, but only if they pray. If they don't pray, not only will they miss the primary goal of their lives, but also they will cut off their source of life.

Mother Teresa was never bashful about the importance of prayer. When the Indian prime minister Jawaharlal Nehru came to see her, Mother Teresa did what she always did when visitors came into the home. Before anything else she took him to the chapel in order to pay respect to the Master of the house. She had the courage to tell this powerful political leader to wait because talking to Jesus was so important.

Mother Teresa made more than short visits of respect to the chapel, however. She spent at least an hour a day in prayer before the Blessed Sacrament. She saw this time as an opportunity to be with Jesus, allowing him to shape her and direct her life through their silent communion. She spoke about her experience: "Often a deep and fervent look at Christ is the best prayer: I look at Him and He looks at me."[16]

Too often we reduce prayer to merely presenting our petitions, hopes, and desires to God. While that is part of prayer, Mother Teresa knew that prayer is more essentially about nurturing our relationship with Jesus. In those moments when she felt the need to use words in her prayer, she believed they should be "burning words coming forth from the furnace of a heart filled with love."[17] The love she had for Jesus, nourished in daily prayer, was a fountain that overflowed into her love for others.

Imitating Mother Teresa's external actions of service without roots sunk deeply in a life of prayer could result in acts of vanity that simply shrivel up. Attempting to model her aura of goodness without a solid foundation of prayer would divorce these admirable characteristics from their source. Loving her neighbors had to flow from first loving Jesus, spending time in his presence, seeking his guidance and grace every single day. She believed, "Action to be productive has need of contemplation."[18]

Recognizing our dependence on prayer is liberating. It frees us from the futile pressure to do difficult things on our own. God's grace will give us the strength we need. By communicating frequently and directly with Jesus, we can love our neighbors as ourselves even when it's a challenge.

Jesus did not leave us orphans when he ascended into heaven. He still gives us access to the grace and assistance we need to overcome our weaknesses. Mother Teresa's prayerful, sacramental life bears testimony to the reality of this grace. So do the thousands of women who have given up everything to live in poverty among the sick and rejected as Missionaries of Charity.

The service of the Missionaries of Charity is entirely Christ-centered. Their love for their neighbors comes from their relationship with Jesus. A life of prayer ensures their essential communication with Jesus and ever deepening love for him. "We must possess before we can give,"[19] Mother Teresa would say.

She also told the members of her order that their vocation was to belong to Jesus. All they did for the poorest of the poor was nothing more than putting into practice their love for Christ. One of her favorite mottoes was "Be only all for Jesus through Mary,"[20] a phrase that encapsulates one of the motivating ideas behind Mother Teresa's life and work. She desired to do everything for Jesus, to help quench the thirst of Christ.

Quenching Christ's thirst. In every chapel of every Missionary of Charity house hangs a large crucifix surrounded by the words "I Thirst" in distinctive black letters. This reminds the sisters of the words Jesus spoke during his moment of greatest need on the cross (see John 19:28). Remembering that Jesus bore this tremendous suffering out of his great love encourages the sisters to make a response. Inspired by their union with Jesus in prayer, they go out into the world and quench his thirst for souls by bringing people to know and accept his love.

In a letter to the members of her order, Mother Teresa wrote:

> For me it is so clear—everything in MC [Missionaries of Charity] exists only to satiate Jesus. His words on the wall of every MC chapel, they are not from the past only, but alive here and now, spoken to you....
>
> The heart and soul of MC is only this—the thirst of Jesus' Heart, hidden in the poor.... Satiating the living Jesus in our midst is the Society's only purpose for existing.[21]

In return for all Jesus had done for her, Mother Teresa longed to bring souls to him. When her cause for canonization began, some of her letters that had been unavailable to the public clarified her reasons for founding the order. She wrote when requesting permission from Archbishop Perier to start the new order, "I have been longing to be all for Jesus and to make other souls...come and love Him fervently...and so love Him as He has never been loved before."[22]

For Mother Teresa, drawing people to Jesus meant offering them lasting happiness and bringing happiness to the heart of Jesus as well. Showing care and compassion to those in need paved the way for them to come to know and love Jesus. Mother Teresa never lost sight of this. Yet she never pressured those she served to accept Jesus in return for the care she gave them. She and her sisters always respected the religious beliefs of the people they took in, even burying people according to their native rites.

In spite of this Mother Teresa faced criticism that she was primarily concerned with proselytizing. Hindu priests, for example, were resistant when she opened a home for the dying close to a Hindu temple. But she ended up winning their respect. When one of their own priests was dying of a contagious disease, no one would go near him except Mother Teresa. She picked him up and carried him to the home so the sisters could care for him. After this the resistance to her work diminished. One Hindu priest went so far as to refer to Mother Teresa as "the goddess Mother."[23]

Her love in action often won over those who initially resisted her. They came to appreciate the wholehearted, free service that she offered without any expectations in return.

When requesting permission to open a home in Ethiopia, for example, the minister of the imperial court questioned her about what she wanted from the government. She said, "Nothing. I have come to offer my Sisters to work among the poor suffering people."

When he asked her what they would do, she replied, "We give wholehearted free service to the poorest of the poor."

The official wasn't sure what to make of Mother Teresa, and he proceeded to inquire about her qualifications. She immediately responded, "We bring love and compassion to the people."

Finally came his one burning question: "Do you preach to the people and try to convert them?"

Mother Teresa's answer: "Our works of love reveal to the suffering poor the love of God for them."[24]

Eventually Mother Teresa opened her home in Ethiopia. Her authentic dedication to love and service had won out.

The gospel the Missionaries of Charity preach is a lived gospel that has power to draw people to Christ without a single word. As Mother Teresa said, "Joy is a net of love by which you can catch souls."[25]

Yet this quiet evangelization never required hiding her faith. She always maintained her simple, unapologetic adherence to Catholic truths. She spoke about them in front of audiences of all religious and political persuasions. Those in her order pray and receive the sacraments daily, and they speak openly about their love for Jesus. Even the walls of their homes for the sick, dying, and abandoned bear testimony to the Person who is at the center of their mission. And day to day, their mission is to find him in the faces of the poor.

The distressing disguise of the poor. Mother Teresa saw Jesus in every child she saved, every leper she cared for, every dying person she picked up off the street. She showed her love for Jesus in the way she loved those around her. This love was inseparable from her life of service and the work of her order.

Mother Teresa always looked for Jesus in "the distressing disguise,"[26] the disguise of the poor, the abandoned, the lonely, and those who are offensive to us. In using the word *disguise*, she acknowledged that such people do not *appear* to be Christ. The poverty, sickness, or anger we see can distract us, hiding the truth about this person at first glance. Mother Teresa challenges us to allow Jesus to cure our blindness by giving us the grace to find him in these unexpected forms.

Mother Teresa's willingness to look past the disguise was at the basis of her work. She never tired of emphasizing Jesus' own promise from the twenty-fifth chapter of Matthew's Gospel. "Christ says: 'For I was hungry and you gave me to eat. I was homeless and you offered me shelter. I was illiterate and you taught me to read. I was alone and you kept me company. You gave me your understanding and your love.'"[27]

The Missionaries of Charity seek to encounter Jesus through their works, loving their neighbors because of Christ's presence among them. Mother Teresa often shared stories of how she and the sisters experienced this in their daily lives.

She frequently told the tale of a young sister who picked a man up off the street one day. This man was in such terrible condition that some skin on his back adhered to the street when she picked him up. His body was full of worms. The sister took him back to the home and lovingly attended to him. After a few hours he died with a smile on his face. When Mother Teresa asked the sister what she felt when she was touching the man's body, the sister replied, "Mother, I've never before felt the presence of Christ, but really, really, I was sure, I was touching his body."[28]

Trusting in Christ's promise that he is present in "the least of these," Mother Teresa relished opportunities to care for the poorest of the poor. Because this was an essential part of the calling God placed on her heart, she decided that those in the order would profess not only vows of poverty, chastity, and obedience but also a fourth vow of wholehearted free service to the poorest of the poor. Those who enter the Missionaries of Charity freely choose to give up their own material comfort in order to live among the poor, sharing their lives and their sufferings. The poor become the sisters' family. For the Missionaries of Charity, the strength to embrace these people as their own—indeed, to love these poor neighbors as themselves—comes from receiving Jesus in Holy Communion.

The Importance of the Eucharist

At daily Mass the sisters glory in the love of Jesus surrounding them. One of the hymns they often sing after Communion explains the belief inspiring their lives:

> My glory and my joy, the myst'ry of our union.
> My Eucharistic Lord now weds my flesh.
> I dwell within His heart for I become a part of Him,
> invaded by His thirst He leads me on.
>
> Invaded by the love of Christ I love my fellow men.
> I tell them of the secrets of His love.
> I live in, with Him, for Him, by Him. He only is my guide.[29]

The lyrics of this song manifest Mother Teresa's teaching that our relationship with Jesus is a two-way exchange. He unites himself to us through the Eucharist (he "weds our flesh"), and then he leads us on, "invaded by His thirst." Mother Teresa did not receive Jesus and his graces selfishly. She gave back to him out of her great love. He satisfied her deepest longings, and then she did her best to satisfy his.

Mother Teresa believed that the union the sisters experience with Jesus in Holy Communion is inseparable from their lives. He himself renews and refreshes them every morning at Mass.

"Our life is linked to the Eucharist,"[30] she would say. She also stated simply that without beginning each day with Jesus in Communion, "we could do nothing."[31]

Mother Teresa's belief in the power of the Eucharist echoes what Christ himself told us: "Truly, truly, I say to you, unless you eat the flesh of the Son of man and drink his blood, you have no life in you" (John 6:53). After some of his disciples questioned the unusual nature of this teaching, Jesus clarified his point: "For my flesh is food indeed, and my blood is drink indeed. He who eats my flesh and drinks my blood abides in me, and I in him" (John 6:55–56).

Mother Teresa understood the Eucharist as a great treasure, a sign of the love Jesus has for us in the present moment. She said, "When we look at the cross, we know how much Jesus loved us. When we look at the tabernacle, we know how much Jesus loves us *now*."[32]

Mother Teresa's profound devotion to the Eucharist is often missing from books and movies about her life, but she frequently made public reference to this great Sacrament. She trusted Christ's words, believing we should weave our lives around the Eucharist if we hope to love our neighbors. She was convinced that it is the same Jesus hidden in the distressing disguise of the poor who gives himself to us in the Blessed Sacrament.

> In Holy Communion we have Christ under the appearance of bread. In our work we find him under the appearance of flesh and blood. It is the same Christ....
>
> ...[I]t is there at the altar that we meet our suffering poor....
>
> ...[I]t is a continual contact with Christ in His work, it is the same contact we have during Mass and in the Blessed Sacrament.[33]

> The Eucharist and the poor are nothing more than the same love of God.... Communion with Christ gives us our strength, our joy, and our love....
>
> ...[W]e need the Bread of Life to know the poor, to love them and serve them.[34]

Mother Teresa accepted the constant Catholic teaching that Jesus is present—body, blood, soul, and divinity—in the Eucharist. Our finite understanding can hardly grasp such an incredible blessing. Through the Eucharist we receive divine, supernatural intervention to help us carry out Christ's will on earth. Mother Teresa believed Christ's physical presence was essential to the concrete situations in her life's work. She knew that she and her sisters could not love as they did without this heavenly assistance.

Joy

Mother Teresa's life of service was a reflection of her love for God. Love and service were inseparable for her. Because love was her motivation, Mother Teresa kept working in spite of many challenges. If she had allowed obstacles to prevent her progress, she would never have ventured out of the convent, started a new order, and cared for so many thousands of people in need.

The adversity she faced was not just external, however. Mother Teresa also dealt with difficult interior trials. She shows us that even in the midst of our miseries and struggles we can act with love.

Thanks to the letters that have become public since Mother Teresa's death, we have gained insights into her faith that only a few trusted confidantes had during her lifetime. We now know that Mother Teresa suffered through an extended period of spiritual darkness. She felt the absence of God's love and struggled tremendously with this feeling of alienation. In a letter to one of her spiritual directors, she wrote about the trials she had been enduring for more than a decade:

> [T]his loneliness, this continual longing for God—which gives me that pain deep down in my heart—Darkness is such that I really do not see—neither with my mind nor with my reason—the place of God in my soul is blank.... I just long & long for God—and then it is that I feel—He does not want me—He is not there. ...I just hear my own heart cry out—"My God" and nothing else comes—The torture and pain I can't explain.[35]

Such intense spiritual suffering came as a shock to many people, because Mother Teresa kept a positive attitude through all of it. She had chosen to continue serving Jesus even in the midst of these trials. She joyfully accepted the call to die to herself daily to help bring souls to Jesus.

What was Mother Teresa's secret? Many times, in meetings and interviews, anxious fans waited with bated breath to hear her give some words of guidance and advice. Often she would offer the simple suggestion to smile at one another. "That's too easy," we might be inclined to think. "Anybody can smile." Perhaps we expect something more significant, dramatic, or challenging from the lips of such a holy woman.

But one of Mother Teresa's charms was her simplicity—not just in her wardrobe and her life but in her whole demeanor. If smiling was the answer to the question, she didn't dress it up to impress people. And as simple as Mother Teresa's words often seem to be, there are layers of depth beneath them.

Smiling, for example, is not always easy. The point of her advice is that we ought to smile even when it's the last thing we *feel* like doing. Mother Teresa proves that this is possible. She once wrote: "My smile is a great mantle which covers a multitude of sufferings. I smile all the time. The sisters and people think that my faith, my hope and my love are profoundly fulfilling me.… If they only knew…only blind faith moves me along, because the truth is that all is darkness for me."[36]

Mother Teresa did not give in to the power of this darkness. She knew she would not be able to show love to her neighbors—and to God—if she allowed herself to become gloomy. She did not pretend life was free of sorrow, but she chose to be joyful in the face of trials.

Once a non-Catholic visitor asked Mother Teresa if she was married, and she replied playfully, "Yes, and I find it sometimes very difficult to smile at Jesus because He can be very demanding."[37] Her simple answer had underneath it the depth of the cross. She felt its demands but freely accepted them without complaint.

Mother Teresa's sisters have learned this lesson. To be in their presence is to see the powerful radiance of continual joy. "What would our life be if the Sisters were unhappy?" Mother Teresa once asked. "Slavery and nothing else. We would do the work but we would attract nobody. This moodiness, heaviness, sadness, is a very easy way to tepidity, the mother of all evil."[38]

The Missionaries of Charity are anything but moody, heavy, and sad; these people are models of cheerfulness. Mother Teresa taught them well: "Cheerfulness is a sign of a generous person. It is often a cloak that hides a life of sacrifice."[39]

The smiles we produce in times of tension, sadness, darkness, and pain—difficult as they may be to conjure at the moment—have a curative effect. These smiles have the power to alleviate and sometimes even destroy misery. One of the best ways to show love to another person is to smile when we might be inclined to scowl. By freely being cheerful, we overcome the slavery of sadness. Making this joyful choice is much easier when the love of God is in our hearts, souls, and minds.

LIVING THE LESSONS

Mother Teresa fulfilled the command to love our neighbors because of her great love for Christ. Everything she did was for him and through him. She expressed it well in these words:

> He is the Life that I want to live.
> He is the Light that I want to radiate.
> He is the Way to the Father.
> He is the Love with which I want to love.
> He is the Joy that I want to share.
> He is the Peace that I want to sow.
> Jesus is Everything to me.
> Without Him, I can do nothing.[40]

But how much she managed to do *with* him! She accomplished all of her work by thinking of it as love in action. "Work without love is a slavery,"[41] she insisted. Studying the life and teachings of Mother Teresa helps us learn how we can cultivate and express this same love for Jesus, putting it into concrete action on behalf of those around us.

Love at Home

When speaking to audiences from wealthy countries such as the United States, Mother Teresa emphasized that we don't have to go to far-off places in order to put love into action. She challenged her listeners to open their eyes and see the needs of their own next-door neighbors and family members. She encouraged people to love those closest to them first.

Mother Teresa believed it is sometimes easier to concern ourselves with the poor who are far away than to turn our attention toward the poor who live right beside us. Many people would prefer to send money to missionaries in India or to go on a mission trip rather than pay a visit to the elderly woman who lives right across the street. There may be a degree of glory associated with exotic, dramatic service, possibly motivating some people to serve for selfish and vain reasons instead of as an act of genuine love.

Although God does call some people to do foreign missionary work, Mother Teresa's words about serving the poor at home teach a valuable lesson: Service is not about glory; it's about love. It's not about doing something humanitarian once a year or every other month; it is meant to be a way of life for every Christian. By opening our eyes to the people around us, we begin to see a multitude of ways we can love our neighbors in our daily lives.

Our neighbors may not be poor materially but rather spiritually or emotionally impoverished. Mother Teresa believed that material poverty is the easiest to deal with: Bread and medicine can alleviate that sort of suffering. The loneliness, alienation, and depression that afflict many people, rich and poor alike, are far harder to cure.

Spiritual and emotional poverty are especially rampant in the Western world. Where money is abundant, there is often emptiness. "Once the longing for money comes, the longing also comes for what money can give: superfluous things, nice rooms, luxuries at the table, more clothes.... [O]ne thing leads to another, and the result will be endless dissatisfaction."[42] Some people may think their dissatisfaction comes from not having enough things rather than from a spiritual void in their lives.

On the other hand, Mother Teresa recognized that those with the greatest material poverty often have incredible riches in other ways.

> I'll never forget one day I was walking down the street and saw something moving in the open drain. I removed the dirt and found a human being there. He had been eaten by worms and, after we had brought him to our house, it took us three hours to clean him. And this man—who lived such a terrible life of suffering in that open drain—only said: "I have lived like an animal in the street, but I'm going to die like an angel, loved and cared for." And just as we were still praying with him, praying for him, he looked up at the Sister and said, "Sister, I'm going home to God," and he died. There was such a wonderful, beautiful smile on his face. I've never seen a smile like that.

> It was so wonderful to see the greatness of a man who could speak like that without complaining, without cursing. Like an angel! This is the greatness of people who are spiritually rich when they are materially poor.[43]

This man was remarkable in his acceptance. He held no grudge or bitterness about his situation.

Mother Teresa believed forgiveness is often a starting point in loving God. "Is there a person who has hurt you?" she asked. "You go and forgive that person. Is there some bitterness? Go and say it is forgiven. And you will find Him. God cannot be found when we are unforgiving."[44]

But even before we forgive others, "Reconciliation begins… with ourselves. It starts by having a clean heart within. A clean heart is able to see God in others."[45] We are called to love our neighbors as ourselves, after all.

Carrying the Cross

Mother Teresa often compared the work she did to the sufferings of Jesus on the cross. She didn't seek to gain pity or to make pretenses of great holiness, but she wanted to love others as Jesus loved her. He loved until it hurt, "to the very limit of love: the cross."[46]

Not one to run from sacrifice and struggle, Mother Teresa embraced it. Striving toward this imitation of Christ freed her to live a life of selfless service. Because she loved Jesus so much, she wanted to share in his passion. She wanted to generously give Jesus whatever he asked of her, and with a big smile.

He may (quietly) ask us to take action that does not come easily or naturally. He may inspire us to visit someone we'd rather not see, to donate something we'd rather not give, or to experience something we'd rather not feel. These requests from Christ invite us to reach beyond our comfort zone and embrace the cross.

If we stop short of loving until it hurts, we miss out on the peace that comes through compassionate, voluntary sacrifice. This peace filled Mother Teresa's life. She believed people all around her were reliving the passion of Christ, and she found tremendous grace by joining in this passion through sharing their sufferings. She considered the opportunity to share in Christ's passion to be a wonderful gift.

It's not difficult to see that we are sharing in Christ's passion when we encounter physical hardship and poverty. But the suffering of Christ was not just physical. He also experienced intense emotional suffering when people rejected, condemned, mocked, denied, and abandoned him. He experienced spiritual suffering as well, which we glimpse in his cry on the cross, "My God, my God, why have you forsaken me?" (Matthew 27:46). Christ's passion embraced all human suffering and impoverishment.

Our own suffering does not always come in dramatic forms. We may encounter small sufferings on a regular basis: the sting of an unkind word, the blow of criticism, the humiliation of being second best. Mother Teresa saw these daily sufferings as opportunities to embrace the cross.

> We often pray, "Let me share with You Your pain," and yet when a little spittle or thorn of thoughtlessness is given to us, how we forget that this is the time to share with Him His shame and pain.

> If we could but remember that it is Jesus who gives us
> the chance through that certain person or circumstance
> to do something beautiful for His Father.[47]

This requires humble acceptance on our part. Mother Teresa gave a simple instruction on how to practice humility in our daily lives:

> Speak as little as possible of oneself.
> Mind one's own business.
> Avoid curiosity.
> Do not want to manage other people's affairs.
> Accept contradiction and correction cheerfully.
> Pass over the mistakes of others.
> Accept blame when innocent.
> Yield to the will of others.
> Accept insults and injuries.
> Accept being slighted, forgotten, and disliked.
> Be kind and gentle even under provocation.
> Do not seek to be specially loved and admired.
> Never stand on one's dignity.
> Yield in discussion even though one is right.
> Choose always the hardest.[48]

Her last line summarizes Christ's call to pick up the cross and follow him. Putting love into action is not the easy route; it's easier to expect someone else to do it or to put it off until later when we have more time, more money, more patience, or more motivation. But Mother Teresa reminds us, "Charity begins today. Today somebody is suffering, today somebody is in the street, today somebody is hungry. Our work is for today, yesterday has gone, tomorrow has not yet come. We see a need, we go to meet it; at least, we do something about it."[49]

If our love for Jesus is sincere, we will not count the cost of loving others, reconciling with them, or serving them. Mother Teresa understood that hard work—and the suffering that comes with it—is part of life. Our devotion to Christ transforms this work and suffering into an act of love. Jesus calls us to pick up our cross and come after him (see Matthew 10:38). We show love in action when we answer this call. Even a small sacrifice made in love is more meaningful than a huge gift made without any sincere generosity.

Generous Hearts

Mother Teresa wanted people to give from their hearts. For some giving money is too easy. When wealthy people wanted to help celebrate the Silver Jubilee of one of her homes, she asked them to prepare and deliver ten meals instead of just giving a financial donation. She said, "Money is not enough.... Give your heart to love and spread love everywhere you go."[50] She urged people not to give from their abundance but to give until it hurts.

Often Mother Teresa would share stories about children who made simple acts of love and sacrifice. One child decided to give up sugar for three days after hearing about a sugar shortage in Calcutta. He filled a small bottle with the sugar he would have normally used and brought the tiny gift to Mother Teresa as an offering for the supplies of the house.

Another child preparing for her First Holy Communion told her parents that instead of a fancy dress and presents in honor of her special day, she wanted to give the money her parents would have spent to Mother Teresa. The love of their daughter moved her father to give up drinking and her mother to stop smoking.

The money they saved ended up being a gift from the whole family, thanks to this child's selfless love.

Mother Teresa also told of a young couple who decided to forgo fine wedding clothes and a wedding feast in order to give a large sum of money to feed the poor. And another woman, who was very wealthy, at Mother Teresa's suggestion began wearing cheaper saris on a regular basis and giving the extra money to the poor. The experience changed this woman's life, because it taught her that in sharing we receive much more than we give.

Mother Teresa's stories were not always of the rich giving to the poor, however. She also liked to tell of the generosity of the poorest of the poor.

Once she hosted a tea party for two thousand children from the slums. The sisters gave each child a little goodie bag holding several special treats. Some children ate only one sweet because they wanted to take the others back to their brothers and sisters at home.

On another occasion, an impoverished mother who received a ration of rice immediately took half of it next door. "They are hungry also," she said.[51]

How can we live out the charity Mother Teresa exemplified, here and now? By putting Christ at the center of our lives and by joyfully rooting ourselves in prayer and the sacraments, particularly the Eucharist. Christ's flesh and blood are the source of our life, and literally consuming them will keep us connected to him.

In turn, loving our neighbors is one of the best ways to show our love for Jesus. When we care for the physical, emotional, or spiritual needs of our neighbors, we are caring for Christ himself.

FOR REFLECTION

- Which of Mother Teresa's qualities do I most admire?
- How could these qualities become part of who I am?

TEN WAYS TO BE MORE LIKE MOTHER TERESA

1. Spend time praying in front of the Blessed Sacrament.
2. Volunteer with an organization that serves the poor or sick.
3. Pray an annual novena to Saint Thérèse of Lisieux.
4. Smile deliberately every day.
5. Visit an elderly widow or widower in your community.
6. Tell one new person a week why you love Jesus.
7. Give up a treasured food or drink each year and donate the savings.
8. Participate in a charitable activity that forces you to step out of your comfort zone.
9. Write to political leaders to ask them to support pro-life, pro-family legislation.
10. Examine your conscience nightly to see if you looked for Christ in your neighbor.

POINTS FOR CONSIDERATION

- Mother Teresa usually got her way. She convinced royalty, presidents, prime ministers, and religious leaders to give her what she wanted, how she wanted it, when she wanted it. But she was not selfish. She asked out of love for her neighbor. She wanted only what served the mission God gave her. She had her way because it was God's way too.

  Consider: How can I more genuinely discern God's will before I set out on a course of action?

- Devotion to the Eucharist enabled Mother Teresa to do what she did. Many people of good will hold her up as a model, but we can't begin to imitate her without fostering a love for Jesus present in the Blessed Sacrament.

  Consider: In what specific ways does the Eucharist impact my daily life?

- Many of us can hardly imagine a person covered with worms, whose flesh is decaying and whose odor is nauseating. But Mother Teresa not only encountered such people every day; she also touched them, held them, and cared for them. She put her own health at risk in order to love Christ in his distressing disguise.

  Consider: When and why have I recoiled from opportunities to serve Christ?

- Voluntary poverty was a source of liberation for Mother Teresa. She believed detachment from worldly comforts brought deeper attachment to Christ. Not only did she own next to nothing, but she lived without even simple comforts like carpet and electric fans. This freed her to experience firsthand that all we need is Christ.

  Consider: What material comforts would be most difficult to give up if God called me to do so?

- Mother Teresa received so much attention that she could have given in to the temptation to consider herself a miracle worker. But she always redirected the attention toward God. She believed she was only an instrument in his hand. Her humility helped make her blessed.

  Consider: How can I respond to compliments for the sake of God's glory instead of my own?

chapter five

※ THE FOUR TERESAS ※

*Stand firm in one spirit, with one mind striving side by
side for the faith of the gospel.*
Philippians 1:27

"How different are the variety of ways through which the Lord
leads souls,"[1] Saint Thérèse once observed. Studying the four
Teresas assures us that there is no rigid mold for sanctity. On the
contrary, these women comprise a colorful collection of personalities, inclinations, backgrounds, and experiences. But in spite
of their differences, they also share some profound similarities.

WHAT'S IN A NAME?

While their common name is not the most impressive connection between these women, it does make a good starting point
for this reflection. The fact that they were all named Teresa was
part of a conscious connection they shared with one another.

Saint Teresa of Avila, as the forerunner of the other three,
obviously had no connection with them during her earthly life.
Her name was simply the baptismal name her parents chose for
her. It was a common name in the region at the time, although
it comes most likely from a Greek word meaning "summer."

Teresa chose to keep this name when she entered the Carmelite
order. Because of her eventual significance in that order and in

the Church, her name is now frequently embellished by phrases like "Our Holy Mother" Teresa and "The Great" Teresa or, as Mother Teresa referred to her, "The Big" Saint Teresa. People usually assume that "Saint Teresa" means Saint Teresa of Avila, and most of the time they're right.

As we have seen, this Teresa was responsible for the reforms that established the Discalced Carmelite order, of which Saint Thérèse and Saint Teresa Benedicta were members. This alone would be enough to associate them with the Great Teresa in a special way. But their bond goes deeper still.

Zélie and Louis Martin named their youngest daughter after Saint Teresa of Avila (Thérèse is the French version of the name). Saint Thérèse recalls in her autobiography how her father used to nudge her during Mass whenever Saint Teresa's name came up. He would lean over and whisper that the priest was talking about her special patron saint.[2]

Thérèse maintained an interest in her patroness throughout her life. She looked to her for inspiration, once telling a priest, "Father, . . . I want to love God as much as Saint Teresa did."[3] She was familiar with many details of Saint Teresa's life, occasionally referencing relevant tidbits in her writing. In her efforts to form novices in the ways of holiness, she consulted a work on the teachings of Saint Teresa.

Thérèse also adorned the wall of her cell at the convent with a picture of Teresa of Avila, and she was inspired by the beloved verse of her patroness, "Forever will I sing the mercies of the Lord."[4] Thérèse employed these words at the beginning of *The Story of a Soul*. She also relished Teresa's famous line from *The Way of Perfection*: "I would give a thousand lives to save one soul."[5]

Saint Teresa Benedicta of the Cross had a special relationship with Teresa of Avila as well. After accepting Christ, but when she was still searching for the fullness of truth, Edith had read the autobiography of Saint Teresa. Within the pages she devoured so eagerly, Edith found what she was seeking. Learning about Saint Teresa of Avila's life not only impelled her to become Catholic, but it also drew her toward her Carmelite vocation.

At the German convent where Edith spent the first years of her religious life, all of the sisters' names began with "Teresia," followed by a second name. But Teresa Benedicta embraced the name for herself with a special devotion and affection. We can gain insight into the influence of Teresa of Avila from a booklet Sister Teresa Benedicta wrote during her first days as a Carmelite entitled *Love for Love: The Life and Works of Saint Teresa of Jesus.*

Sister Teresa Benedicta was influenced by Saint Thérèse as well. She thought very highly of the simple spirituality of the "Little Flower," whose name and ideas appear in several of her writings.

Mother Teresa might seem at first glance to be the outsider of the group, since she didn't enter the Carmelite order. But although she never wore a Carmelite habit, she carried a Carmelite sensitivity in her heart. She understood the impor-tance of coming to love Jesus through prayer, an essential part of Carmelite spirituality. And she took her religious name in honor of Saint Thérèse, whom she affectionately called "The Little Teresa." She kept a picture of Thérèse on the wall of her room. Through her devotion to Saint Thérèse, Mother Teresa was also connected with the other Carmelite doctors of the Church, Teresa of Avila and John of the Cross. Because they influenced Thérèse, they also influenced Mother Teresa's spirituality, her life, and her love for Jesus.

JOINED WITH JOHN OF THE CROSS

Saint John of the Cross, a beloved saint of the Carmelite order, is another link between the four Teresas. He and Teresa of Avila were contemporaries and friends. They worked simultaneously on the reforms of the Carmelite order, sharing many of the struggles, rejections, and hardships of the task. Both of them were mystical writers whose supernatural prayer experiences were similar in many ways. People often consult these two doctors of the Church in tandem as experts on the life of prayer.

The other Teresas did not know Saint John of the Cross personally, but he was nonetheless influential in their lives. Saint Thérèse was strongly attracted to his writings, which are filled with the same poetic passion and love for God that resonated so deeply in her own heart. Even when she ceased to do much other reading, she continued to relish his works. She wrote, "Ah! how many lights have I not drawn from the works of our holy Father, St. John of the Cross!"[6]

Thérèse latched on to many of Saint John's ideas and wove them into her own writings. Mother Teresa knew well such references from *The Story of a Soul*, which introduce the reader to Saint John of the Cross through the eyes of Saint Thérèse.

Saint Teresa Benedicta, too, had a great affinity for Saint John of the Cross. For the holy card that commemorated her profession into the Carmelites, she chose a quote from his *Ascent of Mount Carmel*: "To arrive at being all, desire to be nothing."[7] Her great spiritual work, *The Science of the Cross,* explored the teachings of this holy man. During retreats she loved to meditate on his writings. She found solace and guidance through his exploration of the spirituality of the cross.

Teresa of Avila, Thérèse, and Mother Teresa all had personal experiences with the "dark night of the soul" that Saint John of the Cross explored. Teresa of Avila suffered tremendous doubts and fears even in the midst of some of her greatest spiritual consolations. Thoughts of unworthiness plagued her for a time, as well as the spiritual disease of scrupulosity. Even prayer became a great struggle for her because of these torments. The writings of Saint John of the Cross express how God draws souls nearer to himself through such trials.

Thérèse also experienced the spiritual darkness that Saint John of the Cross so masterfully described. When she was dying of tuberculosis, she no longer felt the sweet company of Jesus or any consolations from her faith, leading to incredible spiritual agony. She was tempted to doubt God's existence, but she continued to make acts of faith, trusting in God even though she couldn't sense his presence. She made deliberate references to Saint John of the Cross, who spoke of a soul being purified by this dark night in order to be consumed entirely by love. Thérèse believed, even in the midst of this spiritual agony, that she was dying of love.

Mother Teresa knew the isolation of spiritual darkness as well. For most of her years of service, she no longer felt the same closeness to Jesus that had led her to begin the Missionaries of Charity. Instead she felt loneliness and doubt. Yet she unceasingly offered herself to Jesus, meeting him every day in the Eucharist and then in the people she served.

For Teresa Benedicta of the Cross, a keen sensitivity to the spirituality of the cross was already present when she chose her religious name. In declaring herself to be "Blessed by the Cross," she acknowledged that the suffering she had already endured and the trials she anticipated were—like the experience of the dark night—ultimately aimed at a deeper union with Christ. As all signs had indicated, the horrors of persecution of the Jewish people only increased during her lifetime. She felt it was her mission to prayerfully bring the light of Christ into this tragic darkness on behalf of those who did not know for themselves the saving power of the cross.

Even in the midst of suffering, all four of these women were happy, peaceful, and filled with the love of God. Suffering is an element of *every* human life, holy or otherwise; there is no escaping it. Some of us deal with more trials than others or feel them more acutely. But none of us live in a world free of disease, destruction, despair, and death. Such is our fallen human condition.

Hence it's not surprising that all four of the Teresas suffered. How they *dealt* with the suffering is refreshing. Instead of becoming bitter or angry, they accepted their trials and offered them back to God. This leads to another point of convergence for these women.

SHARED SURRENDER

All four Teresas believed in the importance of surrendering their lives to God. They all sought to live for God's will, not for their own. This surrender was not just a mental exercise. Through the concrete circumstances of their lives, they recognized God's will being played out, and they responded accordingly. They saw opportunities in their suffering to trust in God precisely when it was a challenge. They recognized the chance to love God unconditionally, not just when he was showering them with consolations.

This total surrender to God's will helped Teresa of Avila bear insults and criticisms as she pursued her reforms. It enabled Thérèse to say she would be just as happy to remain bedridden and ill if that was God's will. Teresa Benedicta could humbly accept the anonymity of life in the Carmelite novitiate because she knew it was where God wanted her to be. And Mother Teresa lovingly embraced diseased and disfigured people because she believed it was God's will that she serve the poorest of the poor.

Thérèse's idea that God always gave her what she wanted, because she always wanted what he gave her, could sum up the attitudes of all the Teresas. They did not live in a state of restless anxiety, constantly searching for God's will as if it were somewhere else. Because of this free surrender, they radiated the divine light of contentment, joy, and peace.

These women smiled sincerely in challenging situations, even when Church authorities were resistant to their plans. They gave the benefit of the doubt to people who were difficult in circumstances that were less than ideal. They freely offered humble, cheerful service to Christ and his Church, with an untiring spirit of generosity. Like Mary, they were full of grace, not full of grumble.

United Through Mary

Devotion to Mary was literally woven into the fabric of the Teresas' lives. Three of them wore the Carmelite habit, an exterior sign of interior devotion to Our Lady of Mount Carmel. The members of the Carmelite order understand the scapular (the topmost piece of their habit) as a physical reminder to call upon Mary in their needs, to contemplate her life and her virtues, and to imitate her. They also show their Marian devotion with the white mantle of Carmel, a symbol of her purity. As for our non-Carmelite, Mother Teresa selected a habit for her order whose only adornment is a stripe of blue, the color symbolizing Mary.

Mary was part of two of these saints' lives in an especially personal and immediate way, because they had lost their earthly mothers at a young age. Saint Teresa of Avila tells us, "[W]hen my mother died…and…. I began to realize my loss, I went in my distress to an image of Our Lady and, weeping bitterly, begged her to be my mother."[8] Saint Thérèse, after mentioning how she was deprived of her earthly mother, wrote "I put all my heart into *speaking* to [Our Lady], into consecrating myself to her as a child throwing itself into the arms of its mother, asking her to watch over her."[9]

Both Teresa of Avila and Thérèse had supernatural visions in which they believed Mary communicated with them. Perhaps they received this unusual grace because of the intimate way they had entrusted themselves to Mary's maternal care.

Although Teresa Benedicta and Mother Teresa didn't experience the same dramatic dependence upon Mary as the other Teresas, they, too, followed her as their guide. Not only did they honor her in their personal lives, but these two Teresas often spoke publicly about Mary, consistently encouraging other women to follow her example.

Devotion to the Mother of God was one of the essential elements that shaped the femininity of the four Teresas. Without ever neglecting their love for her son, all four of these holy women turned to the Blessed Mother to help them along their way. They found in her not only an intercessor (as any good mother is for her children) but also an inspiration. They wanted to imitate this perfect "handmaid of the Lord" who followed God's will so generously.

HOLINESS IN DAILY LIFE

Like Mary, all four of these women knew that God's will unfolds in the events of daily life. They believed that sanctity comes from living an ordinary life with great love. In our age Saint Thérèse of Lisieux has made famous the "little things with great love" idea. But Teresa of Avila, her patron saint, articulated the concept centuries before. In fact, this idea of Saint Teresa of Avila traveled through the centuries into the thoughts of the other Teresas:

Teresa of Avila: "[T]he Lord does not look so much at the magnitude of anything we do as at the love with which we do it."[10]

Thérèse of Lisieux: "Jesus does not demand great actions from us but simply *surrender* and *gratitude*.... He has no need of our works but only of our *love*."[11]

Teresa Benedicta of the Cross: "St. Thérèse of the Child Jesus shows you even in the little details of daily life how one can follow him."[12]

Mother Teresa: "To the good God nothing is little because He is so great and we so small.... Yes, my dear children, be faithful in little practices of love, of little sacrifices...which will...make you Christ-like."[13]

The four Teresas understood that sanctity is attainable by everyone, regardless of their specific situation. We can all follow the commandments that inherently yield holiness in those who follow them: to love God with our whole heart, soul, and mind and to love our neighbors as ourselves. Mother Teresa insisted that everyone can keep these commandments because God cannot command the impossible. Thérèse believed the same, emphasizing that Jesus himself is the one who helps us keep his commandments by acting through us.

Saint Teresa of Avila directly connected the greatest commandments with the pursuit of holiness. She wrote in *Interior Castle* that "true perfection consists in the love of God and of our neighbour, and the more nearly perfect is our observance of these two commandments, the nearer to perfection we shall be."[14] Teresa Benedicta of the Cross felt that these commandments were so important that they could "certainly be a subject worthy of an entire lifetime of meditation."[15] Thérèse said, "[T]he more united I am to Him, the more also do I love my Sisters."[16] Mother Teresa believed that God put the commandment of loving our neighbor on the same footing as the first commandment.

All four Teresas believed that perfect love for God flows into love for our neighbors. Thus the *two* commandments are virtually one. This is why we associate the saints with acts of service and charity toward humanity. Their love for God impelled them to reach out to others. As such, it is a mistake to *reduce* the saints to their acts of service and charity. They wouldn't be models of service if they weren't first models of loving God. Before all else they were immersed in a life of prayer and the sacraments, which connected them continually to Christ.

This, of course, is the most important connection the four Teresas share. They were all models of holiness. They did more than talk about loving God; they put that love into action.

This connection extends beyond these four women, of course. Every saint in history, all the holy men and women who have gone before us, have shared in the experience of loving God and loving others. Now we are invited to join their company by loving God with our whole being and allowing that love to reach to the ends of the earth.

Seek first his kingdom and his righteousness, and all these things shall be yours as well.
Matthew 6:33

Throughout the course of this book, the four Teresas have provided us with wisdom and practical guidance for following the great commandment. We can summarize their relevant insights with four words: *ask, prepare, open,* and *encounter.*

Ask. Saint Thérèse of Lisieux is our model for loving God with the whole heart. To do this, she believes, we need a new heart. She urges us to *ask* Jesus to share his own Sacred Heart with us. Making this petition in trusting confidence is the key to loving God with all of our heart.

Saint Thérèse teaches us, through her little way and her complete confidence in Christ, that God wants to bestow every blessing on us. He wants to help us transform our hearts by planting his own love within us, if we only *ask* him for this divine favor.

Prepare. Saint Teresa of Avila gives us the image of the soul as a castle where Christ takes up residence. But to provide him with a comfortable resting place there, we need to get things in order. We can *prepare* our souls for his arrival by living a life of prayer, overcoming sin, developing virtue, and making a complete surrender to God—handing over the deed to the property so he can move in. When we *prepare* a beautiful mansion for Jesus, he rewards us with the glory of his presence dwelling in our souls.

Open. Saint Teresa Benedicta of the Cross teaches us to love God with our whole mind by *opening* ourselves to the power of the cross, a "paradox" to closed minds skeptical of God's truth. She opened her mind to the vast supernatural truth of the wisdom of God. Scientific and philosophical knowledge, she came to see, are signposts leading to the ultimate knowledge we find in Christ. He alone is the Way, the Truth, and the Life. Truly open-minded people allow their intellectual compass to point the way to God.

Encounter. Joyfully loving our neighbors as ourselves, according to Mother Teresa, is a matter of *encountering* Jesus in them. She met Jesus every day, first in the Blessed Sacrament and then in those she loved and served. If we love God with our whole heart, soul, and mind, we will long to be with him in the sacraments, in our neighbors, and ultimately in heaven.

These four simple words—and the guidelines they summarize —can help us carry out our fundamental task as Christians. When we focus on following Christ's command to love God and neighbor, he will take care of our other needs and concerns, no matter how daunting, how complicated, or how mysterious they may seem to be. He promised this when he said, "Seek first [God's] kingdom and his righteousness, and all these things shall be yours as well" (Matthew 6:33).

May we learn from the victorious examples of the four Teresas that the greatest satisfaction in life does not come from eliminating every struggle, solving every problem, and answering every question. Rather, as Jesus himself assures us, our true fulfillment in this life—and in the next—comes from loving God with our entire being: heart, mind, and soul.

Introduction

1. Joseph Ratzinger, *Being Christian*, David Walls, trans. (Chicago: Franciscan Herald, 1970), p. 40.

Chapter One: Saint Thérèse of Lisieux: Loving God With Your Whole Heart

1. Thérèse of Lisieux, *Story of a Soul: The Autobiography of Saint Thérèse of Lisieux*, John Clarke, trans. (Washington, D.C.: ICS, 1996), p. 27.

2. Thérèse of Lisieux, *Story of a Soul,* p. 168.

3. Francois Jamart, *Complete Spiritual Doctrine of Saint Thérèse,* Walter Van de Putte, trans. (Staten Island, N.Y.: Alba House, 1961), p. 154.

4. Thérèse of Lisieux, *Saint Thérèse of Lisieux: Her Last Conversations,* John Clarke, trans. (Washington, D.C.: ICS, 1977), p. 62.

5. Thérèse of Lisieux, *Story of a Soul,* p. 194.

6. Jamart, p. 107.

7. Thérèse of Lisieux, *Her Last Conversations,* p. 129.

8. Jamart, p. 79.

9. Thérèse of Lisieux, *Story of a Soul,* pp. 197–200.

10. Thérèse of Lisieux, *Story of a Soul,* pp. 207–208.

11. Thérèse of Lisieux, *Story of a Soul,* p. 200.

12. Ida Friederike Gorres, *The Hidden Face: A Study of St. Thérèse of Lisieux,* Richard and Clara Winston, trans. (San Francisco: Ignatius, 2003), p. 253.

13. Thérèse of Lisieux, *Story of a Soul,* p. 72.

14. Bernard Bro, *Saint Thérèse of Lisieux: Her Family, Her God, Her Message,* Anne Englund Nash, trans. (San Francisco: Ignatius, 2003), p. 66.

15. Jamart, pp. 74–75.

16. Conrad De Meester, *With Empty Hands: The Message of Thérèse of Lisieux*, Mary Seymour, trans. (Washington, D.C.: ICS, 2002), p. 101.

17. Hans Urs von Balthasar, *Thérèse of Lisieux: The Story of a Mission*, Donald Nicholl, trans. (New York: Sheed and Ward, 1954), p. 85.

18. Thérèse of Lisieux, *Story of a Soul*, p. 189.

19. Von Balthasar, p. 265.

20. www.crossroadsinitiative.com.

21. Von Balthasar, p. 213.

22. Thérèse of Lisieux, *Her Last Conversations,* p. 253.

23. Thérèse of Lisieux, *Story of a Soul*, p. 237.

24. Thérèse of Lisieux, *Story of a Soul*, p. 41.

25. Gorres, p. 247.

CHAPTER TWO: SAINT TERESA OF AVILA: LOVING GOD WITH YOUR WHOLE SOUL

1. Marcelle Auclair, *Teresa of Avila,* Kathleen Pond, trans. (New York: Pantheon, 1953), p. 13.

2. Teresa of Avila, *The Life of Saint Teresa of Ávila by Herself*, J.M. Cohen, trans. (New York: Penguin, 1957), p. 30.

3. *The Life of Saint Teresa of Ávila by Herself,* p. 31.

4. *The Life of Saint Teresa of Ávila by Herself,* p. 67.

5. V. Sackville-West, *The Eagle and the Dove* (Garden City, N.Y.: Doubleday, 1944), p. 111.

6. *The Life of Saint Teresa of Ávila by Herself,* p. 39.

7. Teresa of Avila, *Interior Castle,* E. Allison Peers, trans. (New York: Doubleday, 1989), p. 32.

8. See Teresa of Avila, *The Way of Perfection,* E. Allison Peers, trans. (New York: Doubleday, 1991), p. 192.

9. *The Life of Saint Teresa of Ávila by Herself,* p. 63.

10. *The Life of Saint Teresa of Ávila by Herself,* p. 78.

11. Teresa of Avila, *Interior Castle,* p. 214.

12. Teresa of Avila, *Interior Castle,* pp. 28–29, 31.

13. *The Life of Saint Teresa of Ávila by Herself*, p. 219.

14. *The Life of Saint Teresa of Ávila by Herself*, p. 148.

15. *The Life of Saint Teresa of Ávila by Herself*, p. 114.

16. *The Life of Saint Teresa of Ávila by Herself*, p. 114.

17. Teresa of Avila, *The Way of Perfection*, p. 188.

18. *The Life of Saint Teresa of Ávila by Herself*, p. 99.

19. *The Life of Saint Teresa of Ávila by Herself*, p. 114.

20. Teresa of Avila, *Interior Castle*, p. 196.

21. Teresa of Avila, *The Way of Perfection*, p. 122.

22. Teresa of Avila, *Interior Castle*, p. 90.

23. *The Life of Saint Teresa of Ávila by Herself*, p. 98.

CHAPTER THREE: SAINT TERESA BENEDICTA OF THE CROSS: LOVING GOD WITH YOUR WHOLE MIND

1. Waltraud Herbstrith, *Edith Stein: A Biography*, Bernard Bonowitz, trans. (San Francisco: Harper and Row, 1985), pp. 3–4.

2. Herbstrith, p. 20.

3. Florent Gaboriau, *The Conversion of Edith Stein*, Ralph McInerny, trans. (South Bend, Ind.: St. Augustine's Press, 2002), pp. 24–25.

4. Edith Stein, *Life in a Jewish Family: Her Unfinished Autobiographical Account*, Josephine Koeppel, trans., vol. 1, *The Collected Works of Edith Stein* (Washington, D.C.: ICS, 1986), p. 2.

5. John Sullivan, ed., *Carmelite Studies: Edith Stein Symposium, Teresian Culture*, "Remarks of the Pope About Edith Stein" (Washington, D.C.: ICS, 1987), p. 301.

6. Sullivan, pp. 302–303.

7. Sullivan, p. 303.

8. Quoted in a 1952 book review by Evelyn Waugh of a biography of Edith Stein by Sister Teresia de Spiritu Sancto, available at www.baltimorecarmel.org.

9. Freda Mary Oben, *Edith Stein: Scholar, Feminist, Saint* (New York: Alba House, 1988), p. 36.

10. www.spiritualitytoday.org.

11. Edith Stein, *Knowledge and Faith,* Walter Redmond, trans. (Washington, D.C.: ICS, 2000), p. 128.

12. Stein, *Knowledge and Faith,* p. 12.

13. Gaboriau, p. 104.

14. Edith Stein, *The Science of the Cross,* Josephine Koeppel, trans., vol. 6, *The Collected Works of Edith Stein* (Washington, D.C.: ICS, 2002), p. 77.

15. Edith Stein, *The Hidden Life: Hagiographic Essays, Meditations, Spiritual Texts,* Waltraut Stein, trans., vol. 4, *The Collected Works of Edith Stein* (Washington, D.C.: ICS, 1992), p. 94.

16. Stein, *The Hidden Life,* p. 102.

17. Stein, *The Hidden Life,* p. 92.

18. Stein, *The Hidden Life,* pp. 92–93.

19. Stein, *The Hidden Life,* p. 120.

20. Stein, *The Science of the Cross,* p. 11.

21. Stein, *The Science of the Cross,* p. 182.

22. Gaboriau, p. 107.

CHAPTER FOUR: BLESSED TERESA OF CALCUTTA: LOVING YOUR NEIGHBOR AS YOURSELF

1. www.catholicnewsagency.com.

2. Edward Le Joly and Jaya Chaliha, eds., *Mother Teresa's Reaching Out in Love: Stories Told by Mother Teresa* (New York: Barnes & Noble, 1998), p. 55.

3. Mother Teresa, *Come Be My Light: The Private Writings of the "Saint of Calcutta,"* Brian Kolodiejchuk, ed. (New York: Doubleday, 2007), p. 40.

4. www.catholicworker.com.

5. Mother Teresa, *Come Be My Light,* p. 48.

6. Mother Teresa, *Come Be My Light,* p. 47.

7. Le Joly and Chaliha, *Mother Teresa's Reaching Out in Love,* p. 25.

8. Le Joly and Chaliha, *Mother Teresa's Reaching Out in Love,* p. 69.

9. Mother Teresa, *One Heart Full of Love,* José Luis González-Balado, ed. (Ann Arbor, Mich.: Servant, 1988), pp. 78–79.

10. www.usatoday.com.

11. Mother Teresa, *The Love of Christ: Spiritual Counsels,* Georges Gorrée and Jean Barbier, eds. (San Francisco: Harper and Row, 1982), p. 93.

12. *Lumen Gentium,* 40, in Austin Flannery, ed., *Vatican Council II: Volume I, The Conciliar and Post Conciliar Documents,* rev. ed. (Northport, N.Y.: Costello, 1996), p. 397.

13. Mother Teresa, *The Joy in Loving,* Jaya Chaliha and Edward Le Joly, comp. (New York: Penguin Compass, 1996), p. 92.

14. Mother Teresa, *No Greater Love,* Becky Benenate and Joseph Durepos, ed. (Novato, Calif.: New World Library, 1997), p. 3.

15. Mother Teresa, *One Heart Full of Love,* p. 57.

16. Mother Teresa, *No Greater Love,* p. 7. Mother Teresa echoes the words Saint John Vianney heard from an elderly man of his parish.

17. Mother Teresa, *The Love of Christ,* p. 111.

18. Mother Teresa, *The Love of Christ,* p. 100.

19. Mother Teresa, *The Love of Christ,* p. 99.

20. www.asianews.it.

21. www.mcpriests.com.

22. Mother Teresa, *Come Be My Light,* p. 47.

23. Le Joly and Chaliha, *Mother Teresa's Reaching Out in Love,* p. 68.

24. Le Joly and Chaliha, *Mother Teresa's Reaching Out in Love,* pp. 72–73.

25. Joan Guntzelman, "Blessed Mother Teresa of Calcutta: The Life of a Saint," *St. Anthony Messenger,* vol. 111, no. 5 (October 2003), p. 34.

26. Mother Teresa, *One Heart Full of Love,* p. 6.

27. Mother Teresa, *One Heart Full of Love,* p. 3.

28. Le Joly and Chaliha, *Mother Teresa's Reaching Out in Love,* p. 26.

29. Program for Profession of Final Vows, Missionaries of Charity, November 21, 2004, National Shrine of the Immaculate Conception, Washington, D.C.

30. Mother Teresa, *No Greater Love*, p. 115.

31. Malcom Muggeridge, *Something Beautiful for God: Mother Teresa of Calcutta* (New York: Harper & Row, 1986), p. 108.

32. www.therealpresence.org.

33. Muggeridge, pp. 74, 108, 114.

34. Mother Teresa, *One Heart Full of Love,* pp. 27, 49.

35. Mother Teresa, *Come Be My Light*, pp. 1–2.

36. Jacques Gauthier, *I Thirst: Thérèse of Lisieux and Mother Teresa,* Alexandra Plettenberg-Serban, trans. (Staten Island, N.Y.: Alba House, 2005), p. 73.

37. Mother Teresa, *No Greater Love*, p. 34.

38. Mother Teresa, *The Love of Christ*, p. 104.

39. Mother Teresa, *The Love of Christ*, p. 104.

40. Mother Teresa, *One Heart Full of Love,* pp. 15–16.

41. Mother Teresa, *The Love of Christ*, p. 84.

42. Mother Teresa, *The Love of Christ,* p. 106.

43. Le Joly and Chaliha, *Mother Teresa's Reaching Out in Love,* pp. 21–22.

44. Le Joly and Chaliha, *Mother Teresa's Reaching Out in Love*, p. 98.

45. Mother Teresa, *The Love of Christ*, p. 95.

46. Mother Teresa, *No Greater Love*, p. 23.

47. Mother Teresa, *The Love of Christ*, p. 88.

48. Mother Teresa, *The Love of Christ*, p. 82.

49. Le Joly and Chaliha, *Mother Teresa's Reaching Out in Love*, p. 35.

50. Le Joly and Chaliha, *Mother Teresa's Reaching Out in Love*, p. 64.

51. Le Joly and Chaliha, *Mother Teresa's Reaching Out in Love,* p. 32.

CHAPTER FIVE: THE FOUR TERESAS

1. Dwight Longenecker, *St. Benedict and St.Thérèse: The Little Rule & The Little Way* (Huntington, Ind.: Our Sunday Visitor, 2002), p. 19.

2. See John Beevers, trans., *The Autobiography of St. Thérèse of Lisieux: The Story of a Soul* (New York: Doubleday, 1957), p. 34.

3. Pierre Descouvemont and Helmuth Nils Loose, *Thérèse and Lisieux* (Grand Rapids: Eerdmans, 1996), p. 131.

4. Descouvemont and Loose, p. 128.

5. Descouvemont and Loose, p. 129.

6. Thérèse of Lisieux, *Story of a Soul*, Clarke, trans., p. 179.

7. Stein, *The Science of the Cross*, p. xx.

8. *The Life of Saint Teresa of Ávila by Herself*, p. 24.

9. Thérèse of Lisieux, *Story of a Soul*, Clarke, trans., p. 78.

10. Teresa of Avila, *Interior Castle*, p. 233.

11. Thérèse of Lisieux, *Story of a Soul,* Clarke, trans., pp. 188, 189.

12. Stein, *The Hidden Life*, p. 108.

13. Mother Teresa, *Come Be My Light*, p. 34.

14. Teresa of Avila, *Interior Castle*, p. 42.

15. Stein, *The Hidden Life*, p. 4.

16. Thérèse of Lisieux, *Story of a Soul*, Clarke, trans., p. 221.

bibliography

Auclair, Marcelle. *Saint Teresa of Avila*. Trans. Kathleen Pond. New York: Pantheon, 1959.

Bro, Bernard. *Saint Thérèse of Lisieux: Her Family, Her God, Her Message.* Trans. Anne Englund Nash. San Francisco: Ignatius, 2003.

Cavnar, Cynthia. *Meet Edith Stein: From Cloister to Concentration Camp: A Carmelite Saint Confronts the Nazis.* Ann Arbor, Mich.: Servant, 2002.

De Meester, Conrad. *With Empty Hands: The Message of St. Thérèse of Lisieux.* Trans. Mary Seymour. Washington, D.C.: ICS, 2002.

Descouvemont, Pierre, and Helmuth Nils Loose. *Thérèse and Lisieux.* Grand Rapids: Eerdmans, 1996.

Flannery, Austin, ed. *Vatican Council II: The Conciliar and Post Conciliar Documents.* Northport, N.Y.: Costello, 1973.

Gaboriau, Florent. *The Conversion of Edith Stein.* Trans. Ralph McInerny. South Bend, Ind.: St. Augustine's Press, 2002.

Garesche, Edward. *The Teachings of the Little Flower.* New York: Benzinger, 1925.

Gauthier, Jacques. *I Thirst: Saint Thérèse of Lisieux and Mother Teresa of Calcutta.* Trans. Alexandra Plettenberg-Serban. Staten Island, N.Y.: Alba House, 2005.

Gorrée, Georges and Jean Barbier, eds. *The Love of Christ: Spiritual Counsels, Mother Teresa of Calcutta.* San Francisco: Harper & Row, 1982.

Görres, Ida Friederike. *The Hidden Face: A Study of St. Thérèse of Lisieux.* San Francisco: Ignatius, 2003.

Guntzelman, Joan. "Blessed Mother Teresa of Calcutta: The Life of a Saint." *Saint Anthony Messenger* 111, no. 5 (October 2003), pp. 30–35.

Herbstrith, Waltraud. *Edith Stein: A Biography.* Trans. Bernard Bonowitz. San Francisco: Harper & Row, 1985.

Jamart, Francois. *Complete Spiritual Doctrine of St. Therese of Lisieux*. Trans. Walter Van de Putte. Staten Island, N.Y.: Alba House, 1961.

John Paul II. *Redemptoris Mater*. Encyclical on the Blessed Virgin Mary in the Life of the Pilgrim Church. Boston: Pauline, 1987.

———. *Fides et Ratio*. Encyclical on the Relationship Between Faith and Reason. Boston: Pauline, 1998.

Koeppel, Josephine. *Edith Stein: Philosopher and Mystic*. Vol. 12, *The Way of the Christian Mystics*. Collegeville, Minn.: Liturgical, 1990.

Longenecker, Dwight. *Saint Benedict and Saint Thérèse: The Little Rule & The Little Way*. Huntington, Ind.: Our Sunday Visitor, 2002.

Mother Teresa. *Come Be My Light: The Private Writings of the "Saint of Calcutta."* Ed. Brian Kolodiejchuk. New York: Doubleday, 2007.

———. *In My Own Words*. Ed. José Luis González-Balado. New York: Gramercy, 1997.

———. *Jesus the Word to Be Spoken: Prayers and Meditations for Every Day of the Year*. Comp. Angelo Devannda. New York: Walker, 1987.

———. *The Joy in Loving: A Guide to Daily Living*. Comp. Jaya Chaliha and Edward Le Joly. New York: Penguin Compass, 1996.

———. *Meditations from a Simple Path*. Comp. Lucinda Vardey. New York: Ballantine, 1996.

———. *No Greater Love*. Eds. Becky Benenate and Joseph Durepos. Novato, Calif.: New World Library, 1997.

———. *One Heart Full of Love*. Ed. José Luis González-Balado. Ann Arbor, Mich.: Servant, 1984.

———. *Mother Teresa's Reaching Out in Love: Stories Told by Mother Teresa*. Comp. Edward Le Joly and Jaya Chaliha. New York: Barnes & Noble, 1998.

Muggeridge, Malcom. *Something Beautiful for God: Mother Teresa of Calcutta*. New York: Harper & Row, 1986.

New American Bible. Saint Joseph edition. New York: Catholic Book, 1970.

Neyer, Maria Amata. *Edith Stein: Her Life in Photos and Documents.* Trans. Waltraut Stein. Washington, D.C.: ICS, 1999.

Oben, Freda Mary. *Edith Stein: Scholar, Feminist, Saint.* New York: Alba House, 1988.

Ratzinger, Joseph. *Being Christian.* Trans. David Walls. Chicago: Franciscan Herald, 1970.

Sackville-West, V. *The Eagle and the Dove: A Study in Contrasts—St. Teresa of Avila, St. Thérèse of Lisieux.* Garden City, N.Y.: Doubleday, Doran, 1944.

Stein, Edith. *Finite and Eternal Being: An Attempt at an Ascent to the Meaning of Being.* Trans. Kurt F. Reinhardt. Vol. 9, *The Collected Works of Edith Stein.* Washington, D.C.: ICS, 2002.

———. *The Hidden Life: Hagiographic Essays, Meditations, Spiritual Texts.* Trans. Waltraut Stein. Vol. 4, *The Collected Works of Edith Stein.* Washington, D.C.: ICS, 1992.

———. *Knowledge and Faith.* Trans. Walter Redmond. Vol. 8, *The Collected Works of Edith Stein.* Washington, D.C.: ICS, 2000.

———. *Life in a Jewish Family.* Trans. Josephine Koeppel. Vol. 1, *The Collected Works of Edith Stein.* Washington, D.C.: ICS, 1986.

———. *On the Problem of Empathy.* Trans. Waltraut Stein. Vol. 3, *The Collected Works of Edith Stein.* Washington, D.C.: ICS, 1989.

———. *Philosophy of Psychology and the Humanities.* Ed. Marianne Sawicki. Trans. Mary Catharine Baseheart and Marianne Sawicki. Vol. 7, *The Collected Works of Edith Stein.* Washington, D.C.: ICS, 2000.

———. *The Science of the Cross.* Trans. Josephine Koeppel. Vol. 6, *The Collected Works of Edith Stein.* Washington, D.C.: ICS, 2002.

———. *Self-Portrait in Letters, 1916–1942.* Trans. Josephine Koeppel. Vol. 5, *The Collected Works of Edith Stein.* Washington, D.C.: ICS, 1993.

———. *Woman.* Trans. Freda Mary Oben. Second edition. Vol. 2, *The Collected Works of Edith Stein.* Washington, D.C.: ICS, 1996.

Sullivan, John, ed. *Carmelite Studies 4: Edith Stein Symposium—Teresian Culture.* Washington, D.C.: ICS, 1987.

Teresa of Avila. *Interior Castle.* Trans. E. Allison Peers. New York: Image, 1989.

—————. *The Life of Saint Teresa of Ávila by Herself.* Trans. J.M. Cohen. New York: Penguin, 1957.

—————. *The Way of Perfection.* Trans. E. Allison Peers. New York: Image, 1991.

Thérèse of Lisieux. *Letters of Saint Thérèse of Lisieux, Volume II.* Trans. John Clarke. Washington, D.C.: ICS, 1988.

—————. *Story of a Soul: The Autobiography of Saint Thérèse of Lisieux.* Trans. John Clarke. Third edition. Washington, D.C.: ICS, 1996.

—————. *St. Thérèse of Lisieux: Her Last Conversations.* Trans. John Clarke. Washington, D.C.: ICS, 1977.

Von Balthasar, Hans Urs. *Thérèse of Lisieux: The Story of a Mission.* Trans. Donald Nicholl. New York: Sheed and Ward, 1954.

Welcome to Carmel: A Handbook for Aspirants to the Discalced Carmelite Secular Order. The Growth in Carmel series. Huburtus, Wis.: Teresian Charism Press, 1998.

Women for Faith & Family. "Affirmation for Catholic Women." *Women for Faith &Family.* www.wf-f.org.

Zaleski, Carol. "The Dark Night of Mother Teresa." *First Things.* May 2003, pp. 24–27.

WEB SITES

www.baltimorecarmel.org: Articles on Carmelite saints.

www.catholicnewsagency.com: Articles on Mother Teresa.

www.catholicworker.com: Teresa of Avila had a profound influence on Dorothy Day, founder of the Catholic Worker movement.

www.crossroadsinitiative.com: Articles on Thérése of Lisieux.

www.mcpriests.com: Official Web site of the Missionaries of Charity Fathers, the religious community of priests founded by Mother Teresa of Calcutta.

www.spiritualitytoday.org: Selected articles from the archives of
Spirituality Today, a Dominican journal of spirituality.

www.therealpresence.org: Real Presence Eucharistic Education and
Adoration Association.

GINA LOEHR holds a master's degree in theology from Franciscan University of Steubenville. Author of *Real Women, Real Saints* and *Choosing Beauty: A 30-Day Spiritual Makeover for Women,* she writes and speaks on such topics as the virtues, the sacrament of marriage, and the vocation of women. Gina lives with her husband, daughter, and baby boy on a six-hundred-acre dairy farm in southeastern Wisconsin.